Daily Encounters

Photographs from Fleet Street

ROGER HARGREAVES

Essay by BILL DEEDES

Daily Encounters

Photographs from Fleet Street

NATIONAL PORTRAIT GALLERY, LONDON

Published to accompany the exhibition
Daily Encounters, held at the
National Portrait Gallery, London,
from 5 July to 21 October 2007.

Supported by

gettyimages®

Published in Great Britain by
National Portrait Gallery Publications,
National Portrait Gallery,
St Martin's Place, London WC2H 0HE

For a complete catalogue of current
publications please write to the
address above, or visit our website at
www.npg.org.uk/publications

ISBN 978-1-85514-377-7

A catalogue record for this book
is available from the British Library.

Publishing Manager: Celia Joicey
Editor: Caroline Brooke Johnson
Copy Editor: Lesley Levene
Designer: Philip Lewis
Production Managers: Ruth Müller-Wirth
and Tim Holton

Printed and bound in the Far East

FRONT COVER: Alfred Hitchcock (detail),
see page 99
BACK COVER: Mandy Rice-Davies and
Christine Keeler (detail), see pages 90–91
FRONTISPIECE: Louis Blériot and Lord
Northcliffe (detail), see page 39

Contents

Foreword   6

Supporter's foreword   8

Preface   11

Illuminating newspapers   12
BILL DEEDES

1   Photojournalism in Fleet Street   16
2   The page makers   38
3   Candid camera   54
4   Breaking and making news   72
5   The end of Fleet Street   100

Index   118
Acknowledgements   120

Foreword

THIS BOOK CHARTS an alternative kind of portraiture that developed over the twentieth century: a portraiture of the street, of public space and interaction within it, of what documentary photographers captured through skill and sometimes guile, as opposed to the art of the photographic studio. The portraits range from those taken at public occasions, including the arrival of heroes and heroines and the collective passion at sporting victories, to private moments caught within the public realm.

The emergence of photography as the predominant form of image making within daily newspapers a century ago was critically important for several reasons. First, it gave a directness to the news, appearing to offer the truth of the event – of what actually happened as it was witnessed – without any editorial interference. Secondly, it gave an immediacy to the recording of the event, instead of being inter- preted in a second-hand form through a reporter's description or the more nuanced processes of drawing or lithography. It allowed you, the reader, to feel something of being there. Thirdly, it caught public figures or unsuspecting subjects off guard, allowing

them to be seen without the ceremony of the photographic studio.

Photographic portraits in newspapers not only changed the news for their readers, but also hold a special place for certain artists, as Walter Richard Sickert recorded in 1934:

> I had an instance that pleased me very much indeed. I painted a portrait of the King and he did not sit to me. I got my material from an instantaneous photograph and by chance Major Featherstonhaugh was standing talking to the King at the time the photograph was taken and neither knew they were being photographed. In those circumstances you get much more information – much more than from an isolated person.

(Walter Richard Sickert, Lecture, November 1934, *Walter Richard Sickert: The Complete Writings on Art*, ed. Anna Gruetzner Robins, Oxford, 2000, p.652)

Whatever the presumption of the street – that documentary photographers capture people as they appear, without their permission – there is a certain element of performance in the appearance of well-known public figures and this has been an arena of changing techniques and possibilities. It is the skill of these photographers that lies behind the intrigue and fascination of the images of *Daily Encounters*.

I should like to thank Roger Hargreaves, formerly Photography Education Manager at the Gallery, who conceived *Daily Encounters* and who has undertaken the research and the selection with great flair. Getty Images have provided invaluable support by providing archival images free of charge, with particular thanks to Sarah McDonald, David Stanley and Matthew Butson. Finally, I am most grateful to Lord Deedes for adding his poignant words at the start of this book. His contribution to Fleet Street over many decades gives him a special place in its history and I am delighted that he should have been prepared to share his thoughts on the importance of its image making and distribution over the past century.

SANDY NAIRNE
Director, National Portrait Gallery

Supporter's foreword

Getty Images is delighted to work in partnership with the National Portrait Gallery on *Daily Encounters*. Our Hulton Archive, with access to over seventy million images from the birth of photography and beyond, is firmly rooted in Fleet Street. We are proud caretakers of such iconic archives as those of *Picture Post*, Keystone Press and the *Daily Express*, whose editors and photographers brought the best of twentieth-century British press photography to the breakfast tables of the nation. Their legacy is a rich visual document of great events and people interwoven against a backdrop of the inconsequential day-to-day and continues to shape our photographic heritage.

SARAH McDONALD
Curator, Hulton Archive, Getty Images

Ken Joy setting a new speed record, London to Brighton, 5 November 1949

Bert Hardy, *Picture Post*

Bert Hardy's career as one of Britain's most accomplished photojournalists began in part through his interest in cycling. Having responded to a 'boy wanted' notice, at a West End photography printers, he spent what he could save from his wages on a bike and a camera. After working for the General Photographic Agency he set up his own agency, Criterion Press, in a rented office with a darkroom at 172 Fleet Street before becoming a staff photographer with *Picture Post* in 1941. Realizing the potential of sport to attract new readers, the *Daily Express* sponsored the first Tour of Britain between 1951–1955.

Front page, 1 October 1938 (OVERLEAF)

Daily Sketch

The headline 'Peace for Our Time' and the image of a paper-waving Prime Minister Neville Chamberlain have become fused as a captioned icon of modern history. In fact the photograph and the statement were made at two separate locations. Chamberlain provided the visual moment as he stepped off the plane at Heston airport to wave the peace accord jointly signed by Adolf Hitler to a phalanx of photographers and reporters. Later that day, while surrounded by cheering crowds outside Downing Street, he contributed the defining phrase, 'I believe it is peace in our time.'

DAILY SKETCH

No. 9,177   SATURDAY, OCTOBER 1, 1938   ONE PENNY

PREMIER SAYS 'PEACE FOR OUR TIME'—P. 3

Give Thanks In Church To-morrow

TO-MORROW is Peace Sunday.

Hardly more than a few hours ago it seemed as if it would have been the first Sunday of the most senseless and savage war in history.

The "Daily Sketch" suggests that the Nation should attend church to-morrow and give thanks.

THE fathers and mothers who might have lost their sons, the young people who would have paid the cost of war with their lives, the children who have been spared the horror of modern warfare—let them all attend Divine Service and kneel in humility and thankfulness.

To-morrow should not be allowed to pass without a sincere and reverent recognition of its significance.

MR. CHAMBERLAIN SHOWS THE PACT AT HESTON

'Never To Go To War Again'

WHEN Mr. Chamberlain arrived at Heston last night he said:

"This morning I had another talk with the German Chancellor, Herr Hitler. Here is a paper which bears his name as well as mine. I would like to read it to you:

"'We, the German Fuehrer and Chancellor and the British Prime Minister, have had a further meeting to-day and are agreed in recognising that the question of Anglo-German relations is of the first importance for the two countries and for Europe.

"'We regard the agreement signed last night and the Anglo-German Naval Agreement as symbolic of the desire of our two peoples never to go to war with one another again.

"'We are resolved that the method of consultation shall be the method adopted to deal with any other questions that may concern our two countries and we are determined to continue our efforts to remove possible sources of difference and thus to contribute to the assurance of peace in Europe.'"

(Here are the signatures on the pact)

September 30, 1938.

Preface

ROGER HARGREAVES

The words 'Fleet Street' still evoke the British newspaper industry, lingering on like the taste of a warm beer long after the glass has been drained and the pub emptied. The tightly knit geographic base for British newspapers, whose pavements literally shook with the vibrations of the giant presses, has moved on. By the 1980s 'Fleet Street' began to unravel, pitching itself high up into the gleaming Manhattan-style towers of Canary Wharf, its offices strung out among the new purpose-built factories dispersed throughout the old London docks.

Modern newspapers, read by mass audiences, were a phenomenon that first appeared at the very end of the nineteenth century. Like many of the great innovations of the industrial age, they were the commercial evolution of an established practice and took root quite naturally in the enclave of London that had been the specialist centre of printing for 400 years. In the eighteenth century, between bouts of depression and the mania of writing the first dictionary, Samuel Johnson frequented the area's coffee shops and taverns, trading gossip in a manner and style that would be mirrored by latter-day journalists.

Daily Encounters examines the making of the myth of modern British newspapers by relating the story of newspaper photography as one very particular strand of Fleet Street journalism. As the book and the exhibition it accompanies have been commissioned by the National Portrait Gallery, the narrative is inexorably drawn towards the tussle over the iconography of public figures, both the politically established and the transiently famous.

In many ways the press photograph is the very antithesis of the National Portrait Gallery's stock-in-trade – the delicately negotiated magazine studio portrait and the gilt-framed canvas soaked in unctuous oils. Press photographs, illuminated by a sunburst of harsh flash, present an altogether less forgiving gallery of portraits. And yet mention any one of the most celebrated personalities from recent British history and we are as likely to remember a grainy newspaper image as we are a colour-saturated Beatonesque pose. The truth is that public iconography, for over a century the near-exclusive preserve of photography, is a seamless weave of hard-news imagery, private snaps and the softer profile of commissioned magazine portraits, tempered by flickering clips of television and film.

Photographs that were once here for only a day have lived on, brought back from the twilight world of archives to remind us that history was once shockingly fresh.

Illuminating newspapers

BILL DEEDES

Glance at any quality newspaper before 1900. There are long unleaded columns of close type, reporting what public men have said and done, but no impression of what they looked like. The *Daily Graphic* (founded in 1890) was the first morning picture paper, but in its earliest years it was illustrated by the drawings of artists rather than photographs. We owe a lot to Alfred Harmsworth (later Lord Northcliffe) for brightening up newspapers. His *Daily Mirror*, relaunched in 1904, was at first a failure, but his *Daily Mail*, which had been launched in 1896, was an immediate success and a pathfinder in newspaper photography. Today, a photograph occupying much or even the whole front page is seen by most newspapers to be indispensable.

A striking photograph can be more eloquent than prose – and sometimes tell us more about character. There was a photograph taken early in the last century of David Lloyd George and Winston Churchill as relatively young men walking towards Parliament (right). Both are wearing silk top hats and smart dark clothes. Churchill carries a silver-topped walking stick. The photograph not only conveys the character of both men, but offers an impression of Parliament in those days.

Photographers then wielded heavy box cameras, which used plates. They were hard work, and their transmission slower than it is today, with modern cameras from which pictures can be transmitted as quickly as the reporter's story, off a computer.

Churchill was a brilliant illustration of the photograph's power. What he said during the Second World War created an immense impression, but it was enhanced by photographs of what he looked like. Was it not the outstanding Canadian photographer Yousuf Karsh who, when photographing Churchill, set up his camera but, before clicking the shutter, stepped forward and gently removed the cigar from the Prime Minister's lips? The result was a portrait of Churchill looking magnificently belligerent and an inspiration to all engaged in the war. Whether legend or fact, it is a story that deserves to be believed.

There is an early photograph of Stanley Baldwin as Conservative Prime Minister, which well conveys the sort of man he was. Baldwin is wearing a stiff white wing collar and tie and a long tweed jacket and is holding a cherry wood pipe (page 14). Here you see a wealthy industrialist, devoted to the countryside and anxious to convey to the public his genuine feelings for rural England.

**Prime Minister Stanley Baldwin with
his wife, Chequers, Buckinghamshire,
1 November 1924**
Unknown photographer

**David Lloyd George and Winston
Churchill on budget day, London,
27 April 1910** (PREVIOUS PAGE)
Central Press

Photographs can influence events. During the long silence that preceded the abdication of King Edward VIII, during which the British public knew virtually nothing of his close association with Mrs Simpson, a photograph appeared of them on holiday in Yugoslavia (below). It set tongues chattering. But it is happier photographs of the royal family that remain in the mind's eye. One of them is the look on the face of King George V during his Silver Jubilee as he drove down the Mall amid cheers from an enormous crowd. A modest man, he was bewildered by the affection being shown towards him. There is another striking photograph of Queen Elizabeth, the Queen Mother, on the balcony of Buckingham Palace during celebrations marking the fiftieth anniversary of the Second World War's end in 1995. It embodies much that some of us recall from those war years: steadfastness, courage, and on the darkest days a reassuring smile.

These are impressions that even a skilled portrait painter would find hard to convey. Hardest of all would be painting a fair impression of Diana, Princess of Wales, in her various moods. That takes us to the controversial side of newspaper photography, which is what some regard as its invasion of privacy. No question, photographs that catch celebrities in embarrassing situations fetch a high price from some newspapers. That is what keeps a tribe of photographers known as the paparazzi in business. With all accusations of excess by newspapers, however, it is well to remember the observation of Alexis de Tocqueville in his classic *Democracy in America*:

> So where the press is concerned, there is not in reality any middle path between licence and servitude. To cull the inestimable benefits assured by freedom of the press, it is necessary to put up with the inevitable evils springing therefrom.

That view of the press is hard to swallow when one recalls the death of Diana, chased through Paris by the paparazzi, some of whom took photographs of her dying moments in the car that had crashed. One of them appeared recently in an Italian newspaper. Yet those of us who have encountered dictatorships in which the press is severely censored know that de Tocqueville had a point for both photographers and reporters.

Sharp photographs illuminate newspapers. As William Berry (later Viscount Camrose) found when he took over a pretty drab *Daily Telegraph* in 1928, they also help to sell newspapers. More than that, they help to illuminate in the reader's mind the men and women who govern the country, and others who influence society. They serve democracy.

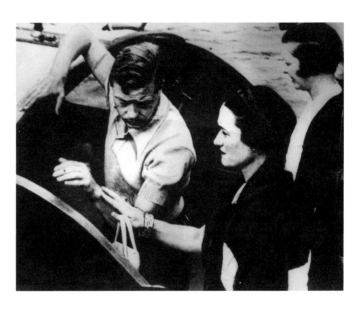

King Edward VIII with his fiancée Mrs Wallis Simpson on holiday in Yugoslavia, August 1936
Keystone Press

1 Photojournalism in Fleet Street

Photography has always been painfully conscious of its lowly status among the visual arts, a neurosis compounded by the stated ambition of the National Portrait Gallery on its foundation in 1856: to inspire portrait artists 'to soar above the mere attempt at producing a likeness, and to give that higher tone which was essential to maintain the true dignity of portrait painting as an art'. Undoubtedly 'the mere attempt at producing a likeness' was meant to encompass the emergent practice of photography, the invention of which had first been announced in 1839 and which, by 1856, was fast encroaching on the established market of portrait engravings. Over the years, photographers have responded to their feelings of insecurity by delineating a fiercely hierarchical caste system, filtering down from the pure-art photographer, through the more successful commercial practitioner, to the press photographer and street trader firmly rooted at the foot of the ladder.

Always conscious of social and cultural pecking orders, Cecil Beaton, that supreme snob of British photography, was forever seeking to distance himself from the rank and file 'pressman'. In his diaries of the Second World War, he recounted how, when documenting the impact of the Blitz on London, he had carefully framed St Paul's Cathedral in the smoke and ruins of a burnt-out shop:

> Through the arch could be seen, rising mysteriously from the splintered masonry and smoke, the twin towers of the cathedral. It was necessary to squat to get the archway framing the picture. I squatted. A press photographer watched me and when I gave a surly look, slunk away.
>
> (Cecil Beaton, *The Years Between: Diaries 1939–1944*, Weidenfeld & Nicolson, 1965)

To this imagined insult came professional injury, for when Beaton returned 'from lunch with my publisher, my morning's pictures still undeveloped in my overcoat pocket, I found the press photographer's picture was already on the front page of the *Evening News*'.

Press photography rapidly emerged as a new form of trade following the appearance of the relaunched *Daily Mirror* as the world's first photographically illustrated newspaper in January 1904. The invention of the half-tone print process in the late nineteenth century had made the reproduction of photographs in newspapers a possibility. The *New York Daily Graphic* first attempted this in 1880, but the technique was not widely applied until the 1900s, after

EXETER (Daily) GAZETTE.

GREENOCK (Evening) TELEGRAPH.

BACUP | TORQUAY TIMES. | TIMES.
CONNACHT TRIBUNE.
CONNACHT SENTINEL
STANDARD (Dublin.)
Buenos Aires Herald.

SURREY MIRROR

H. R. TADGELL.

which it became a significant and essential ingredient of the popular press.

The first incarnation of the *Daily Mirror* had appeared a year earlier, in 1903, as a paper edited by women for women and was launched with a free promotional hand-mirror. The brainchild of the prototype press baron Alfred Harmsworth, the title crashed spectacularly, nose-diving from a first-day circulation of 276,000 to a low of 24,801. Harmsworth drafted in an army of tried and trusted male newspaper hacks to salvage the title and try out something different. They were led by editor Hamilton Fyfe, whose first job was to brush aside the little presents and notes begging to be retained that had been left on his desk and sack the women staff who had put them there, an experience he described with unconcealed relish as 'like drowning kittens in a sack'. Foremost among his team was Hannen Swaffer – later billed as the first art editor on Fleet Street – who was charged with redesigning the paper and incorporating photography into the mix. In his introduction to the autobiography of leading newspaper photographer James Jarché, Swaffer recalled how 'a new species of being had invaded Fleet Street':

In those [early] days, the press photographer was regarded as an animal almost beneath contempt. Where he had come from, nobody knew. Often he had owned a small business as a photographer somewhere in the suburbs, one he had thrown up for the high adventure of Fleet Street.

(Hannen Swaffer, Introduction to James Jarché, *People I Have Shot*, Methuen & Co., 1934)

With modest wages but generous expense accounts, the possibility of travel and unprecedented access to key public figures and decisive moments of history, press photographers began to style themselves as social chancers driven by competition and fuelled by intrigue. They swapped gossip, moved from agency to agency and alternated between hunting in packs and working alone in search of the ever elusive scoop.

In the first decade of the twentieth century a mixture of established and new titles adopted photography as their own and crowded into the market. These included the *Daily Mail*, *Daily Express*, *Daily Chronicle* and *Daily Herald* (founded in 1912 by a partnership of trade unionists and socialists and later reborn as the *Sun*). As the popular press proliferated, the need for a constant supply of

**Photographer in Downing Street,
London, 17 November 1911**

Topical Press Agency

Seen here skulking among the crowds, an
Edwardian photographer covers a suffragette
demonstration in Downing Street. Photographers were initially regarded as journalistic
inferiors, as though producing a photograph
was somehow less skilled or creative than
crafting a text. They emerged, sometimes
from running suburban studios, to forge a
new role in a branch of journalism that had
no precedent and therefore brought with
it no heritage.

**Newspaper boy with *Titanic* headline,
London, 16 April 1912** (OVERLEAF)

Topical Press Agency

The sinking of the British luxury liner
Titanic after hitting an iceberg south of
Newfoundland was one of those rare news
stories that are both instantly momentous
and enduringly compelling. The ship that
was billed to be unsinkable duly sank on its
maiden voyage *en route* to New York, with
the loss of just over 1,500 lives. After the
initial shock, newspaper readers were kept
in thrall as first the survivors' stories emerged
and then two official inquiries reported, one
conducted by a special committee of the
US Senate and the other by the British Board
of Trade.

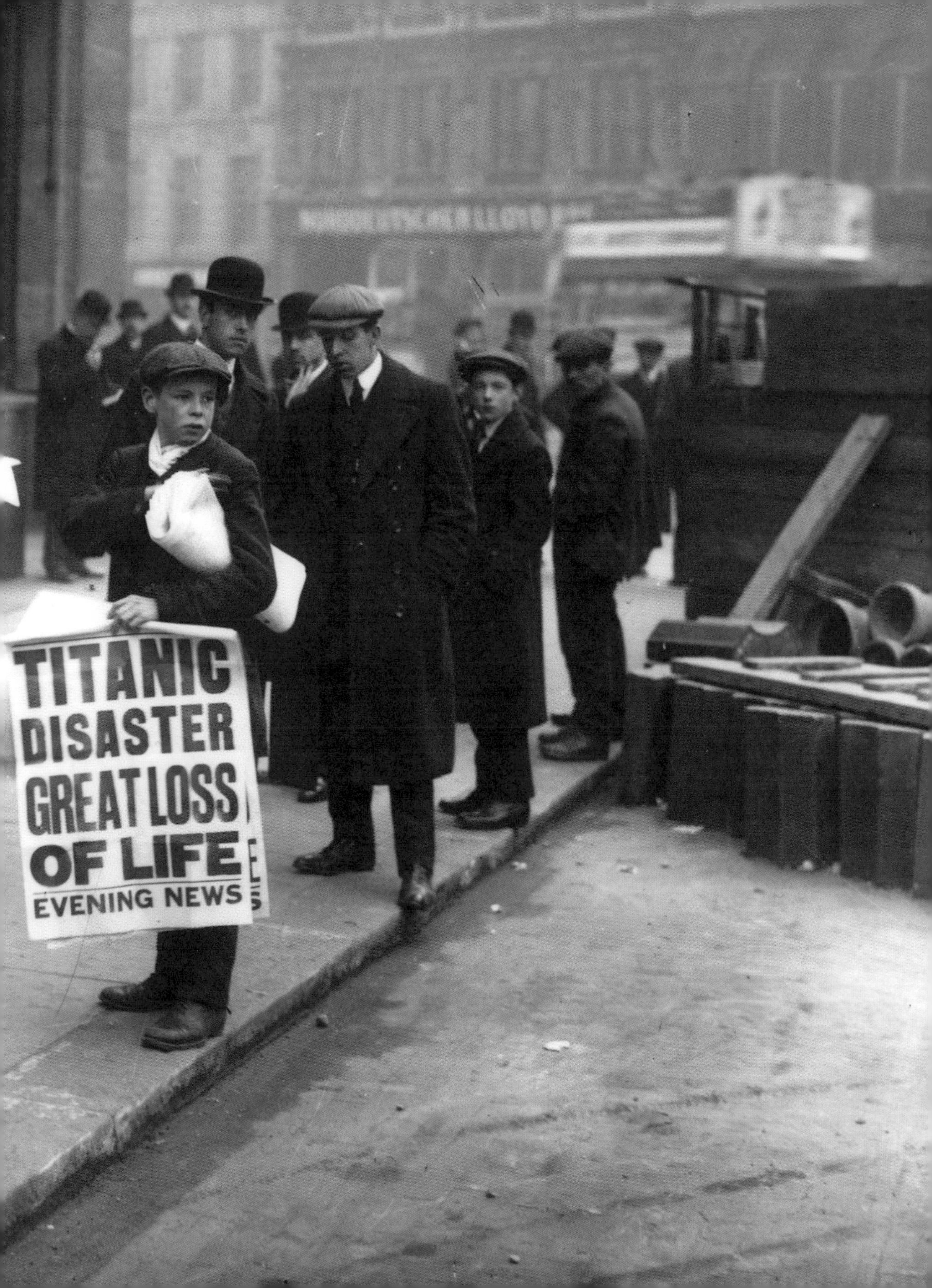
TITANIC
DISASTER
GREAT LOSS
OF LIFE
EVENING NEWS

photographs gave rise to a welter of photographic press agencies, with firms such as Topical, Fox Photos and World Wide beginning to cluster around the newspaper offices and factories in Fleet Street.

The papers were catering for the tastes of a newly literate mass audience. In Britain, the Elementary Education Act of 1870 was the first in a sequence of education reforms that created universal schooling and with it a new generation equipped with the basic skills of literacy. The blend of photographs, headlines and clearly written copy proved potent and circulation among the broad swathe of wage earners rose steadily. Press images became some of the most socially inclusive forms of photography, counterpointing photographs of celebrities and the ruling aristocracy with those of ordinary people, often taken by photographers from their own social class.

Newspaper photography, swelling in frequency and scope, and smuggling in occasional gems hidden in the routine luggage, was quickly changing the opinions and tastes of a mass audience. As the historian Eric Hobsbawm wrote:

For the twentieth century, it was increasingly clear, was the century of the common people, and dominated by the arts produced by and for them. And two linked instruments made the world of the common man visible as never before and capable of documentation: reportage and the camera.

(Eric Hobsbawm, *Age of Extremes: The Short Twentieth Century 1914–1991*, Michael Joseph, 1994)

**Ipswich Town football players in
the communal bath, Ipswich,
11 January 1939** (OPPOSITE)

Daily Express

Between the two world wars professional
football developed into the predominant
spectator sport in Britain, with the largest
crowds attracted to the knock-out drama of
the FA Cup. But for all football's popularity
and commercial success, the players' wages
were capped and they were paid relatively
little. On the other hand, they were accessible
to the public through the press, with whom
they mixed easily, and their individuality
was allowed to shine through, unfiltered
by agents and PR advisers. In 1961 the
maximum £20-a-week wage was abolished
and the Fulham and England centre
forward Johnny Haynes became the
first player to earn £100 a week.

**Reporter at a football match,
12 January 1933**

H.F. Davis, Topical Press Agency

Britain's first telephone exchange opened in
1879, serving just eight subscribers. By the
time the Post Office took over what had
become the National Telephone Company in
1912, there were over half a million users and
a network of public and private phones and
local exchanges linked by trunk lines. The
technology had a profound impact on many
aspects of Britain's social and commercial
life and was felt particularly keenly in the
sphere of journalism. Reports could be
written in shorthand and dictated over
the phone, ensuring both immediacy and
greater accuracy.

**Emigrés registering at
Golders Green, London,
5 September 1939**

William Vanderson, Fox Photos

While many Jewish people from central and
Eastern Europe sought entry into Britain
in the 1930s, just 50,000 were admitted up
until 1939. Both the government and the
established Anglo-Jewish community feared
mass immigration might fuel anti-Semitism.
Unless they arrived with viable businesses
or had work as domestic servants, refugees
were admitted on condition that they did not
seek employment without permission of the
Ministry of Labour. Jewish refugees were
granted residence on a temporary basis,
but were expected to assimilate into British
culture and were actively discouraged from
speaking German in public.

The accompanying article didn't identify the drug being used, but the Second World War fuelled rapid developments in the less benign applications of science and medicine. The Office of Strategic Services, the predecessor of the CIA, began experimenting with LSD in 1943 and the Nazis had been studying the effects of mescaline on inmates at the Dachau concentration camp. As recently as February 2006 Britain's own intelligence service MI6 began to pay compensation to servicemen who underwent experiments on the effects of LSD at Porton Down in the early 1950s.

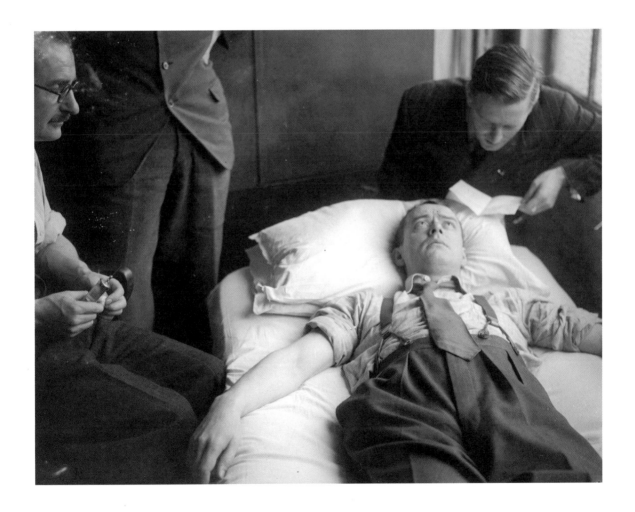

**100-metre dash, London Olympics,
31 July 1948**

Olympic Press Association

The Olympic Games, suspended since those
in Berlin in 1936, were held for the first time
after the war in London. Tokyo was to have
been the venue in 1940, but was replaced by
Helsinki when war broke out between Japan
and China. Then in 1939 Finland was invaded
by the Soviet Union and the obstinate
International Olympic Committee (IOC)
had to bow to the inevitable. In London
the 100-metre dash was won by US hurdler
Harrison 'Bones' Dillard in a race decided by
a photo finish. The technology, evolving from
experiments with multiple cameras to record
motion made by Eadweard Muybridge in
the 1870s, had previously been used only in
horse and greyhound racing.

'Did It Happen?' *Evening Standard* delivery trucks, London, 1954
(PREVIOUS PAGE)
Alex Dellow, *Evening Standard*

Since the turn of the century newspapers have helped to boost their circulation by serializing thrillers and romances. In 1952 the *Evening Standard* invited an eclectic mix of writers, including John Creasey, C.S. Forester, Elspeth Huxley and William Saroyan, as well as the comedian Benny Hill, to craft a short story around the title 'Did It Happen?' The collection was later published in book form.

Press coach at the Monte Carlo Rally, 1954
Alex Dellow, *Picture Post*

The press junket, when the largesse of events organizers could be enjoyed, was a perk of life on Fleet Street. One of the characters in Michael Frayn's 1967 novel *Towards the End of the Morning* describes such a 'facilities trip': 'I'm doing it for a load of crap called *Leisure and Pleasure*.... They don't pay much, but what the hell? It's a week off from the stinking office, with nothing to do but collect a few pix from the firm, slap some sort of crap together from the handout, and get some serious drinking done.... Charge some exes up, of course. Charge a few more up to the paper. It all adds up.'

Merle Oberon press conference, Savoy Hotel, London, 3 April 1956

Jack Esten

The press conference quickly emerged as the most convenient way for celebrities and dignitaries to address, in one go, the swelling numbers of newspaper reporters and photographers. By the 1950s it had become a contractual obligation for visiting Hollywood stars to give an hour of their time to the local press. For photographers the events could be neatly woven into their busy schedules, during which they would photograph five or six stories a day.

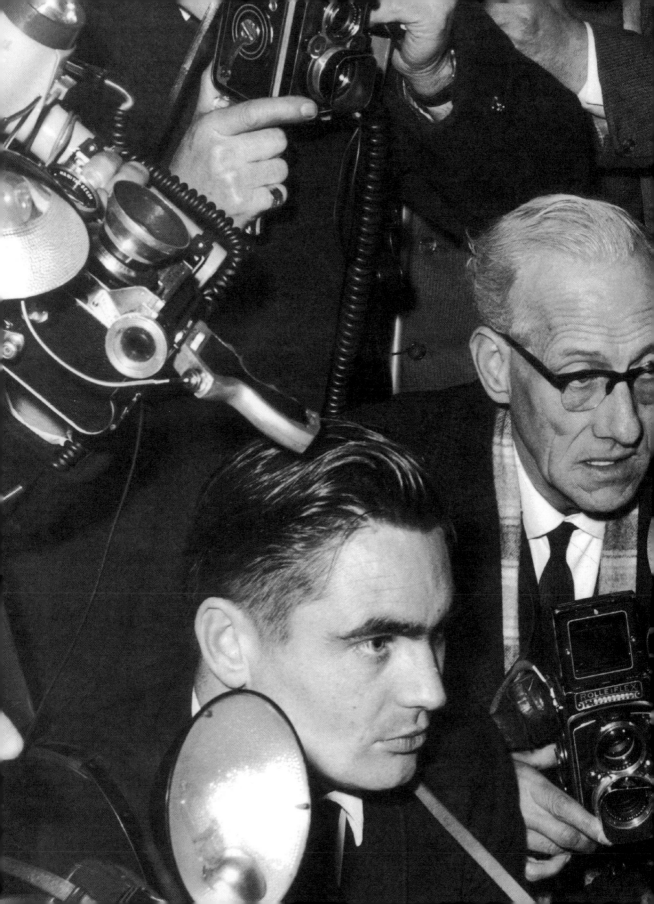

Ringo Starr arriving for a tonsil operation, London, 1 December 1964
(PREVIOUS PAGE)
Fox Photos

Ringo Starr had just completed the 1962 summer season at Butlins, Skegness, as drummer with Rory Storm and the Hurricanes when he was persuaded to join the Beatles. As the group enjoyed meteoric success in 1963, Starr collapsed from tonsillitis and pharyngitis. The troublesome tonsils were eventually removed, to much press interest, in December 1964. Bob Dean (centre) of Associated Press and Frank Hudson (right) of the *Daily Mail* are two of the many photographers who tried to capture the event. A BBC radio newscaster managed to get things wrong by announcing, 'And finally, Ringo Starr's toenails have been successfully removed.'

Model and hatter, London, 9 May 1960
Terence Donovan, *Daily Mail*

Terence Donovan was one of the new wave of working-class fashion photographers in the 1960s who took time out from the pages of *Vogue*, *Nova*, *Queen* and *Man About Town* to work for the popular press. Together with David Bailey, he had trained under John French, the principal fashion photographer for the *Daily Express* and *Daily Mail*. French instilled in him an ability to create not only singular, punchy images that would work within the limited spreads of a newspaper but also large, seductive prints that would grab the attention of the picture editor.

**Harold Wilson and reporters on
the Isles of Scilly, 10 August 1965**

Peter King, Fox Photos

Labour Prime Minister Harold Wilson carefully
cultivated the image of working-class boy
made good. Not for him Edward Heath's yacht-
ing trips to Cowes. He invited the British media
to join him during his summer break as he sat
on a cliff top, puffing his pipe, gazing wistfully
out to sea. Recently released files reveal that
he contacted MI5 to voice concerns that while
on holiday he was being monitored by Russian
ships disguised as trawlers. Hailed as one of
the most brilliant minds in modern politics, he
resigned in 1976, possibly having detected the
onset of Alzheimer's. He died in 1995 and is
buried on the Isles of Scilly.

**Peter Sellers at his divorce hearing,
London, 8 March 1963** (OPPOSITE)

Harold Clements, *Daily Express*

In 1963 Peter Sellers made four films, including
the first in the Pink Panther series. He also
began divorce proceedings against his first
wife, the actress Anne Howe. Celebrity divorces,
involving nobility and actors, were a regular
feature of the early popular press. In 1926
the Judicial Proceedings Act was introduced,
banning the publication of 'indecent' medical,
surgical or physiological information. Prior
to this, as adultery or cruelty had to be established as grounds for a divorce, high-profile
cases were reported in all their salacious detail,
providing Fleet Street with some of the most
sensational stories of the Edwardian era.

2 The page makers

The first edition of *Picture Post*, dated 1 October 1938, just after Chamberlain's meeting with Hitler in Munich, posed a crucial question: who owns the press? For many of its readers, the magazine came to evoke an idealized Albion of working men, rolling hills and wartime defiance. However, while on the outside it might have appeared to be the essence of Englishness, on the inside its principal architect and founding editor, Stefan Lorant, was Hungarian and its first two staff photographers were German. Lorant was part of the wave of émigrés from Germany and Eastern Europe who arrived in London in the 1930s and quietly remodelled the landscape of British culture. Press photography in particular seemed to attract talented Hungarians, at least three of whom came to control the most prosperous post-war picture agencies: Bert Garai at Keystone Press Agency, Tom Blau at Camera Press and Paul Popper at Popperfoto.

Like many of the culturally astute émigrés, Lorant nursed an outsider's curiosity for his newly adopted home. He wanted to know how Britain was fashioned and how it functioned. More crucially, he wanted to know who owned what. So it was announced, '*Picture Post* will publish every week an authoritative survey of a great national institution. This is No. 1. The Press.'

The extensive feature profiled the eight daily national newspapers published in London, outlining their histories, finances, market share and editorships. First to be introduced, beneath their stamp-sized head-and-shoulders photographs, were the chairmen and proprietors: Major John Astor (*The Times*), Lord Camrose (*Daily Telegraph*), Lord Kemsley (*Daily Sketch*), John Cowley (*Daily Mirror*), Sir Walter Layton (*News Chronicle and Star*), Esmond Harmsworth (*Daily Mail*), Lord Beaverbrook (*Daily Express*) and Lord Southwood (*Daily Herald*). Taking a snapshot of newspaper ownership at any one point in the twentieth century would provide a similar complex mix of majority shareholders, outright owners and elected chairmen of trustees. The patterns of control in 1938 ranged then, as now, across the spectrum of influence and experience. The independently wealthy Astor maintained a hands-off approach to both the day-to-day management and the editorial direction of *The Times*. The Lords Camrose and Kemsley were brothers from South Wales who had built from nothing a vast empire of magazines and local and national newspapers which, by 1938, they had divided between them. Cowley and Layton were journalists who had worked their way up through the managerial ranks.

**Louis Blériot and Lord Northcliffe
returning to London, 25 July 1909**
Topical Press Agency

Ably abetted by photography, newspapers
learned to make the news, not just report it.
In 1906 Lord Northcliffe's *Daily Mail* offered
a prize of £1,000 for the first cross-Channel
flight. Three years later French aviator Louis
Blériot finally won the Channel Challenge.
Northcliffe and a large crowd, encouraged by
the *Daily Mail*, greeted his arrival at Victoria,
from where he was driven to a celebratory
lunch at the Savoy. Encouraged by rising
newspaper sales, the *Daily Mail* promptly
offered £10,000 for the first flight between
London and Manchester.

Lord Southwood was the errand boy made good who controlled the Odhams publishing group, while Harmsworth was, by contrast, the Eton-educated heir of Lord Rothermere. From among them Beaverbrook stands out as the highest-profile proprietor and as someone who most closely fitted the popular perception of a press baron, exerting influence from ownership while caring passionately about the craft of popular journalism.

The prototype model was the American William Randolph Hearst, joined in 1941 by his fictional *doppelgänger*, Charles Foster Kane. Orson Welles concocted his cautionary tale of the newspaper magnate, *Citizen Kane*, from the lives of a number of American entrepreneurs, including Howard Hughes. However, Hearst was the one routinely fingered as the most likely source of inspiration and he returned the compliment by offering the production company, RKO Pictures, $800,000 to destroy all prints of the film and burn the negatives.

Hearst rose to prominence in the late nineteenth century, devising sensational journalism for a populist market of new readers. The more aloof *New York Press*, pinched by the circulation battles between 1895 and 1898 of Joseph Pulitzer's *New York World* and Hearst's *New York Journal*, dubbed the work of its competitors 'Yellow Journalism'. While they refused to elaborate other than to add, 'We call them Yellow because they were Yellow,' some believe the origins of the term lie with the Yellow Kid cartoon strip, a popular morsel that Pulitzer and Hearst fought over, outbidding one another for publication rights.

Hearst urged his editors to generate 'headlines that would bite the public like a bulldog'. Photographs came later. One of the most direct references to Hearst in *Citizen Kane* is the mouthing of his alleged comment, 'You provide the pictures and I'll provide the war.'

The local British version of the American media baron emerged with two brothers, Alfred and Harold Harmsworth, later ennobled as Lord Northcliffe and Lord Rothermere. Alfred's ennoblement came despite having taunted his detractors with the quip, 'When I want a peerage I shall buy it like an honest man.' In 1888 they joined forces to publish a weekly magazine, *Answers to Correspondence*, to which readers were invited to send questions. All of these were answered by post, with the most interesting being published in the magazine. Within four years the Harmsworths were selling a million copies a month.

In 1894 Alfred Harmsworth bought the near-bankrupt *Evening News*. With headlines such as 'Was It Suicide or Apoplexy?' and 'Hypnotism and Lunacy', together with a cleaner design and illustrations to break up the text, he turned it around within two years, achieving sales of 800,000 and a profit of £50,000 a year. But his great innovation proved to be the launch of the *Daily Mail* in 1896. Unashamedly based on American newspapers, it favoured shorter, punchier articles under page-wide banner headlines. News was sacrificed in favour of human-interest stories, sport and serialized fiction. Sold under the slogan 'The Busy Man's Newspaper', it also printed pages of fashion and cookery for what it perceived as the interests of a growing market of women readers.

Flattered by the sincerity of the imitation, Joseph Pulitzer invited Alfred Harmsworth to usher in the twentieth century by editing the New Year's Day edition of *New York World*. Harmsworth rose to the occasion by shrinking its size and producing in the process the world's first tabloid newspaper.

His relaunch of the *Daily Mirror* in 1904, after its failed first incarnation as a women's paper, added photography as the final and essential ingredient to the mix of the modern newspaper. Arkas Sapt, one of Harmsworth's technicians, has been credited with devising the technique of printing half-tone pictures at speed on a Hoe rotary press capable of generating 24,000 picture pages an hour. Every major paper quickly followed suit. Circulation of what had become known as the *Illustrated Daily Mirror* steadily improved, trebling to 70,000 on launch and then doubling again within a month. However, Harmsworth's heart was never truly in the title and he sold the *Daily Mirror* to his brother Harold for £100,000 in 1914.

The Harmsworths were just two of a small group of players who, for the next thirty years, traded shares and ownership of newspaper titles like so many poker chips, with the Astors, Cadburys and Pearsons ducking in and out of the tables, dropping and collecting money on a whim and with passion.

While in the right circumstances and under the right management newspapers could generate considerable profits, they equally provided for their owners entrance to the higher-stake gamble

**Amy Johnson arriving at
the *Daily Express* offices,
London, 1 December 1932**

Daily Express

Aviation captured the spirit of modernity
popular newspapers were keen to embrace.
English aviator Amy Johnson's triumphant
return after her record-breaking solo flight
to Cape Town coincided with the recent
opening of the *Daily Express*'s black glass,
art deco offices and printing presses in
Fleet Street. The building, designed by
architects Ellis and Clarke, was an extension
of the title's proprietor, Lord Beaverbrook:
dark and hard on the outside, complex and
labyrinthine within.

of political power and influence. This proved a seductive game and created some big-name casualties. During the First World War, Lord Northcliffe had been appointed Director of Propaganda. As a long-time supporter of Lloyd George, he had assumed that he would be invited to join the British delegation at the Versailles Peace Treaty negotiations. When the invitation proved elusive, he galvanized his newspapers to turn on and attack the government. In a speech to the House of Commons, Lloyd George theatrically tapped his finger to his forehead and accused Northcliffe of suffering the 'disease of vanity'. It proved a devastating putdown. By the time of Northcliffe's death in 1922, the disease had run its full course. He was by then

clinically paranoid, taking some solace from his growing collection of Napoleon memorabilia, while keeping a loaded revolver under his bed, convinced he was the target of German agents.

From beyond the grave Northcliffe had one last surprise for his former employees. He had left instructions for a sizeable portion of his wealth to be used to provide each of his 6,000 staff with an additional three months' salary. Seventy years later, Robert Maxwell came to fit snugly into the mythologized template of the newspaper baron Northcliffe had created: acquisitive, aggressively competitive, delusional and ultimately tragic. The aftertaste for Maxwell's employees was, however, appreciably different.

**Lord Beaverbrook and
Lord Rothermere, Cherkley Court,
Surrey, 30 July 1935** (OPPOSITE)
Unknown photographer

While Lord Northcliffe treated the arrival of
Max Aitken (ennobled as Lord Beaverbrook
in 1917) on the British newspaper scene with
suspicion, his brother Lord Rothermere was
more welcoming. The two press barons
developed a close friendship that encom-
passed business and political interests, with
Rothermere lending support to Beaverbrook's
private and unfulfilled goal of becoming prime
minister. The two were photographed, from
a deferential distance, deep in conversation
at Cherkley Court, the country house from
which Beaverbrook ran his business empire,
surrounded by Dictaphones, ticker-tape
machines and banks of telephones.

**Lord Beaverbrook addressing shop
stewards, Albert Hall, Manchester,
1 January 1941**
David E. Scherman, Time & Life Pictures

Lord Beaverbrook was adept at mixing politics,
finance and newspapers. He served as Minister
of Information during the First World War,
while simultaneously building up the *Daily
Express*. Despite having made conciliatory
gestures, through his newspapers, to Nazi
Germany, once war became inevitable he
lent the government the full weight of his
support. He was appointed Minister of Aircraft
Production under Churchill and guided the
development of bomber and fighter planes.
In 1941 he addressed an audience of 2,000
mostly left-wing shop stewards in an effort
to increase productivity.

Women relaxing with papers, London, 1953 (PREVIOUS PAGE)

Bert Hardy, *Picture Post*

The popularity of newspapers rose steadily from the turn of the century, peaking at the end of the Second World War, when Britons were consuming 15 million a day. The habit was ingrained and the advent of television in the 1950s failed to diminish its appeal. Instead newspapers responded by claiming for themselves some of their rival's territory, moving downmarket with shorter articles, bigger photographs and more content from the growing transient and fickle world of show business.

Keith and Viv Nicholson, pools winners, London, 27 September 1961

Unknown photographer

In September 1961 Castleford miner Keith Nicholson and his wife, Viv, scooped £152,319 on the Littlewoods football pools (the equivalent of around £3 million today). When asked by reporters what they were going to do with the money, Viv announced her intention to 'spend, spend, spend', instantly providing copy for the next day's headlines. A sizeable chunk of their winnings went on cars and in 1965, aged just twenty-seven, Keith was killed at the wheel of his Jaguar. What was left of their by now diminished fortune disappeared in death duties.

Model and newspaper van, London, 1966 (OPPOSITE)

John Cowan

Eager to appeal to women and younger readers, from the early 1960s popular newspapers began to feature a new style of fashion photography by a new breed of fashion photographer. The names David Bailey, John Cowan and Terence Donovan became as familiar to readers of the *Daily Mirror* and *Daily Mail* as they did to readers of *Tatler* and *Vogue*. Cowan's career conformed to the familiar 1960s morality tale: a sensational rise followed by a drink-fuelled crash. His studio was hired by director Michelangelo Antonioni to double as the fashion photographer's studio in his 1966 film *Blow-Up*.

On 5 November 1991 Robert Maxwell was reported missing from his yacht, *Lady Ghislane*, while cruising off the Canary Islands. His body was subsequently discovered, bloated and floating in the Atlantic Ocean. He had died in the most suspicious of circumstances. Within days news of the awful truth about his crumbling business empire and his attempts to shore it up with raids on the Mirror Group Newspapers pension fund began to circulate. It was an ignoble end to a colourful career. He had been born Jan Ludvik Hoch in Czechoslovakia and many of his Yiddish-speaking family perished in the Nazi invasion of his country. He escaped to Britain, joined the British Army, was promoted to the rank of captain (for which he was later mercilessly lampooned by *Private Eye* as Cap'n Bob) and was awarded the Military Cross. Maxwell finally fulfilled his ambition of diversifying into newspapers on the strength of a profitable academic publishing business and a chequered career as a Labour politician.

'Rosebud' is the last word whispered from the deathbed of Orson Welles's fictional Citizen Kane. The search for its meaning becomes the device that carries forward the film's narrative. Those looking for Maxwell's elusive 'Rosebud', the apparently incidental trifle that might betray an underlying truth, should be directed to Watford and the *Mirror*'s printing press. To the side of the paper's extensive and historic photographic picture library is a room with the look and feel of chaotic abandonment. Filing cabinets spill across the floor as if they have been hurled with violence into the empty space. This is the Robert Maxwell Archive. In one corner is a collapsing tower of storage boxes that reaches from floor to ceiling. Each box is packed tight with photographs of Maxwell meeting and greeting everyone of apparent power or potential influence who ever crossed his path. It transpires that Maxwell had two staff photographers on twenty-four-hour call wherever he was in the world. Whenever an aspiring Labour politician, a modestly successful football manager, an East European despot or, as happened, Mother Teresa stepped into his circle, the photographers were ready to record Maxwell's 'grip and grin'. The images, few of which were ever published, are as compelling as they are repetitive and banal, a teetering monument to an ensnaring and insatiable vanity.

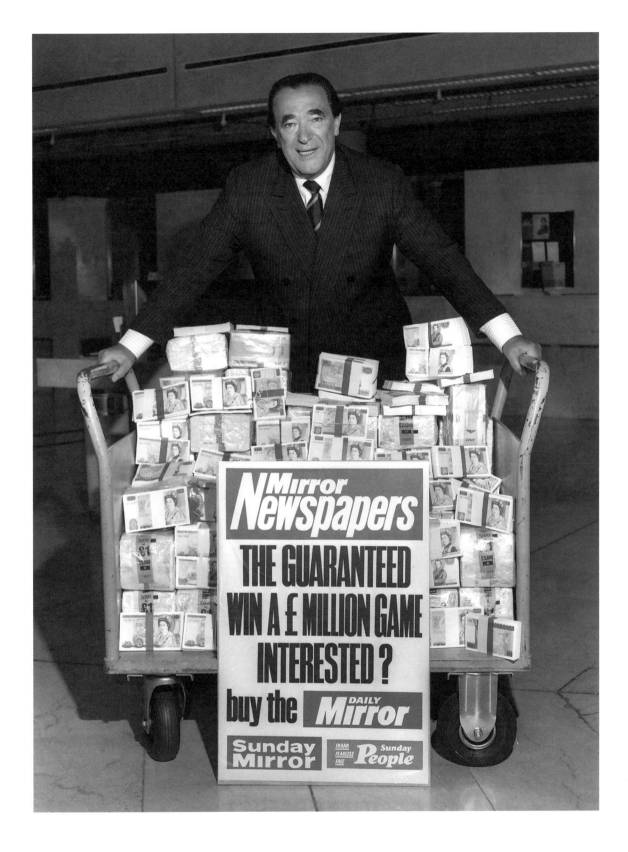

3 Candid camera

Photography had been an agent of celebrity long before photographs began to appear in newspapers. From the late 1850s studio portraits published as cartes-de-visite were issued in serialized part-works alongside anodyne letterpress biographies, widening the pool of the famous and deepening its waters. Generals, scientists, writers and entrepreneurs thrashed around in the deep end, while theatrical stars, socialites and sportsmen paddled the shallows.

Populist newspapers, styled on Hearst's and Pulitzer's 'Yellow Press' (page 40), were instinctively drawn to celebrity and were, by nature, less reverential and more gossipy. Once introduced, photography was set on an inevitable trajectory, becoming intrusive and harsher. Edwardian Britain was ready to express new cultural attitudes through a new medium and parallel developments in camera technology, together with improvements in photographic chemistry, eased the way for the newspapers. Cameras were becoming increasingly versatile and emulsions more sensitive and faster.

By the 1890s 'snapper photography', with imported detective cameras, was breaking free of the constraints of the studio. Paul Martin, whose family had fled France at the time of the Paris Commune, bought one of the new 'Facile' cameras in 1892, carrying it through the streets of London disguised as a parcel wrapped in brown paper. Martin was in an ideal position to understand the possibilities of news photography through his work as a woodcut engraver, translating photographs into magazine illustrations in the era before half-tone reproduction. A pioneer of documentary photography and a publicist for the plight of the urban poor, he depicted the richness of an unselfconscious street life oblivious to his spying eye. He ventured beyond the capital, where he photographed street vendors, vagrants, fairgrounds and funeral crowds, to the south and east coasts. On the beach at Yarmouth he photographed a couple in a passionate embrace beneath a sun umbrella.

The rival American 'Demon Detective' camera was marketed with an eye to similar opportunities: 'on the promenade and railway carriages; also in Breach-of-Promise and Divorce cases: in fact, at all awkward moments when least expected'. Photography was ready to go out and about, free to intrude into privacy and erode the niceties of social division.

The camera initially best suited to press photography was the German Goerz Anschütz strut folding camera, introduced in 1896. It had been designed by Ottomar Anschütz, who, when not photographing

In the garden of his house in Wandsworth, David Lloyd George poses for the newspaper photographer beside his wife and daughters, the very model of the family patriarch and emergent political figurehead. In 1911, when Chancellor of the Exchequer and five years before becoming prime minister, he employed Frances Stevenson as Megan's governess. Two years later Stevenson was promoted to the role of personal secretary and mistress. After agreeing to two abortions she gave birth to a daughter of her own in 1929. The couple married in 1943, two years after Margaret's death.

The dramatic mid-Atlantic arrest of Dr Crippen as he fled to Canada was followed by shocking details of his wife's murder and the disposal of her body. Crippen was said to have burned her limbs in the kitchen stove, dissolved her organs in acid in the bathtub and packed her head in a handbag which he jettisoned on a day trip to Dieppe. During the trial at the Old Bailey photographers packed the courtroom with cameras concealed in their hats, masking the shutter noise with a cough. The coughing became so bad that the judge threatened to clear the press benches and banned photography from the courtroom. This ban eventually became law with the 1925 Criminal Justice Act.

storks in flight and near-naked javelin throwers, served as court photographer to Kaiser Wilhelm II. His string-blind camera had shutter speeds of 1/1000th of a second, but it was cumbersome, the blinds were prone to jamming and it used half-plate glass negatives, which were both heavy and fragile. Photographers often had just two or three plates for each story. They needed to get their picture first time and seldom had the luxury of changing plates.

To make it to the page, each glass plate had to travel with the photographer, be exposed in the camera and then be couriered back to the newspaper office. It might still be ruined at the final moment if, as sometimes happened, a rival photographer had tipped the darkroom assistant to turn the light on at the wrong time. There was one final trial for the shattered nerves of the photographers as they gathered within earshot of the cruellest of the early art directors, who edited by tipping the rejected negatives into a bin.

The press quickly settled on the subject matter that was guaranteed to be of interest to the public:

politics, entertainment, sport, crime and, of course, royalty. On the 2 April 1904 the *Daily Mirror* published a whole page of photographs of Edward VII and his children, George, Louise, Victoria and Maud. Circulation peaked and an unholy alliance was born. While the first royal spread had been of reverential studio portraits, Edwardian royalty soon found themselves trailed by the new breed of news photographers. Edward VII complained that he could 'scarcely venture out of doors without a battery of cameras ready to photograph him' and hated being, as he described it, 'snapshotted'. Photographers were encroaching onto the Sandringham estate while the royals hunted, smuggling themselves into bread delivery trucks to photograph their children and stalking them at the racecourse.

While it might have seemed to the royals that 'the lower classes' were moving ever closer, newspapers were never out to debunk but rather to construct recognizable and essentially benign caricatures. As Tom Hopkinson, the former editor of *Picture Post*, pointed out in an essay on royalty and the newspaper photographer:

If daily life had to be reported in terms of the appropriate cliché, how much more was this true of royalty, the very centre of tradition? To the photographer of that era, the clichés were guide rules to success. 'What's the picture?' a camera-man would ask upon leaving for an assignment. There was seldom any doubt. Everyone was after the same shot: Edward VII bowling smoothly to Epsom or Ascot; George V on the moors with his gun raised, or at the helm of his yacht; the Prince of Wales, hesitant, dressed with a desperate elegance as though clothes would somehow see the job through.

(Tom Hopkinson, *Happy and Glorious: 130 Years of Royal Photographs*, National Portrait Gallery, 1977)

Royal advisers quickly understood that there was mutual benefit in parading their charges before the press, and if they could control the access and direct the image so much the better. The photo opportunity became an accepted part of public life. It was the logical response to the demands of the newspapers and to the practical constraints on photographers' time and materials. By the late 1920s, when the assembled packs were becoming increasingly unwieldy and the inevitable elbowing for best position often turned the atmosphere ugly, the press rota system was introduced. A selected handful of photographers were given access on a rotation basis on the understanding that their pictures would be made available to rival newspapers. The system, still in place today, satisfied the routine demands of the papers while opening a crack for the occasional 'off message' scoop.

The unspoken understanding between royalty and the press persisted until at least the 1980s, coming unstuck only once with the abdication crisis of 1936. The owners of the national newspapers had reached a gentlemen's agreement not to discuss Edward's determination to marry American divorcee Wallis Simpson, despite the fact that the story was being widely reported in Europe and America. When matters finally came to a head, the press were divided about whom to support, with many of the popular titles, including the *Daily Mirror*, *Daily Mail* and *Daily Express*, backing the incumbent royal. When public opinion swung in favour of the estab-lishment view that Edward should go, the papers appeared to lack both journalistic independence and the common touch. This salutary lesson that their principal responsibility was to their readership was one that few editors or proprietors would forget

George V on Derby Day at Epsom, pursued by a beggar, 2 June 1920
Central Press

The Epsom Derby, a flat race for thoroughbred horses, has been held for over 200 years and has developed into one of the fixed points of the British sporting calendar. It has also emerged as a unique social hub, attracting a diverse spectrum of racegoers. The Central Press photographer who caught the moment a beggar ran beside the royal carriage would have understood that he was not only recording the extremes of wealth and power but also encapsulating the essence of Epsom.

The Prince of Wales at Epsom Races, 1 June 1927

Central Press

As the 1920s roared on, Edward, Prince of Wales, cemented his reputation as the debonair and worldly heir to the throne. The press were only too happy to collude in reinforcing a public image of movie-star proportions. The more disquieting aspects of his character passed without comment, to be revealed only in the wake of the crisis following his abdication in 1936.

The Duke of York, Bookham Fair, 1922 (OPPOSITE)

Daily Graphic

A delicate child with a severe stammer, Albert Frederick Arthur George Windsor, known as Bertie to his family, grew up in the shadow of his brother, the Prince of Wales. In 1920 he was created Duke of York and encouraged to enter the world of royal duties and public engagements. The press were keen to create a readily recognizable and benign image and his appearance on a fairground carousel at Bookham Fair, accompanied by spats-wearing attendants, would have contributed to the embryonic newspaper stereotype.

in a hurry. Their photographers were given licence to turn the tables on Edward. The fond images of Prince Charming evaporated away, to be replaced by pictures of a skulking and disgraced royal. The most iconic, taken at night as the Prince was driven from the palace slumped in the back of a car (page 62), had a grabbed and grainy quality that was appreciably different from the precision of earlier pictures shot on glass plate.

By the 1930s small-format, roll-film Leica and Ermanox cameras were appearing from the Continent. Magazine editors like Stefan Lorant, together with the new wave of Hungarian picture agency directors, were actively encouraging a new spirit of photojournalism. The cameras were lighter and quicker, could be used in low light without flash and enabled photographers to make multiple exposures on long strips of film. At first press photographers were sneeringly resistant to these 'toy cameras', dismissing them as a gimmick and deriding their inferior picture quality. However, attitudes began to shift with the impact of Lorant's magazines, beginning with *Weekly Illustrated*. He opened the way for the use of informal and compositionally dynamic photographs and sequential picture stories in place of single images.

Edward VIII Sails at 1.45 a.m. After Poignant Farewell Broadcast

MIDNIGHT DASH TO PORTSMOUTH

His Last Words to The People

"COULD NOT CARRY ON WITHOUT THE WOMAN I LOVE"

"She Tried to the Last To Dissuade Me"

AFTER his farewell broadcast from Windsor Castle at 10 o'clock last night, Edward VIII., accompanied by his equerry, Colonel the Hon.

Prince Edward—until yesterday King Edward VIII.—motoring away from Windsor Castle after his farewell broadcast.

THE BROADCAST IN FULL

"It May Be Long Before I Return"

Edward VIII. in making his farewell broadcast, from Windsor Castle last night, was introduced to the microphone by Sir John

QUEEN MARY'S MOVING APPEAL TO THE NATION

Distress That Fills A Mother's Heart

QUEEN MARY last night addressed the following message "to the people of this Nation and Empire" from Marlborough House :

I have been so deeply touched by the sympathy which has surrounded me at this time of anxiety that I must send a message of gratitude from the depth of my heart.

The sympathy and affection which sustained me in my great sorrow less than a year ago have not failed me now, and are once again my strength and stay.

I need not speak to you of the distress which fills a mother's heart when I think that my dear son has deemed it to be his duty to lay down his charge, and that the reign which had begun with so much hope and promise has so suddenly ended.

I know that you will realise what it has cost him to come to this decision ; and that, remembering the years in which he tried so eagerly to serve and help his country and Empire, you will ever keep a grateful remembrance of him in your hearts.

I commend to you his brother, summoned so unexpectedly, and in circumstances so painful, to take

---

**Edward VIII abdication feature,
12 December 1936**

Daily Mail

The news of Edward VIII's affair with American divorcee Wallis Simpson had been suppressed by the British press. Within a week of the story breaking, Edward had been forced to abdicate the throne. Edward's fall from grace was dramatically underlined by the treatment of his photographic image in the press. Gone were the fondly selected shots of a matinée idol, playboy Prince. In their place appeared the harsher, flash-lit pictures of a prince slumped in the back of a car as he was driven away from Windsor Castle.

**Stanley Baldwin and Ramsay
MacDonald, London, 26 August 1931**

Erich Salomon

In 1927, at the age of forty-one, Erich Salomon used a hidden camera to take photographs in a Berlin courtroom. Within a year his work began to appear in German magazines and then in publications across Europe and America. Using the new, small-format Ermanox camera, he brought readers closer to the public figures who were shaping world history. His photograph of former political adversaries MacDonald and Baldwin announcing the formation of a coalition government perfectly distilled the essence of their uneasy and unlikely partnership.

**Charlie Chaplin strolling along
the Embankment, London,
21 September 1931**

Fox Photos

Pursuing celebrities has always been an
accepted part of press photography. While
the 1931 Fox photographer had none of the
advantages of long lenses, he would have
been working with a relatively large glass
plate negative. This meant he did not have
to come in too close to his subject and the
editor could then crop in tight. Chaplin
had made his first triumphant return from
Hollywood to his native London in 1921.
Ten years later he was back again, this time
to promote *City Lights*, arguably the last
great silent film.

Fleet Street was equally taken with the possibilities opened up by Dr Erich Salomon, an apparently mild-mannered, middle-aged German Jewish lawyer. He first came to prominence in 1928, when he published in the *Berliner Illustrierte Zeitung* a set of pictures taken at an international summit in Switzerland. He had used the discreet small-format camera to take informal shots of European ministers as they went about their business. The images caught the body language and gestures of diplomacy as it was performed by the most powerful in hotel lobbies and over dinner. The photographs were the antithesis of the posed groupings routinely offered to the press and drew the magazine's readers into the inner sanctum of real politics. His pictures began to appear in British magazines and newspapers. Variously dubbed 'the Houdini of Photography', 'the Master of Indiscretion' and 'the Invisible Cameraman', he preferred the label 'Historian with a Camera'. He was essentially a photographer of politics, fascinated by the human dynamic of world events and acutely aware of the significance of the unfolding dramas of the 1930s. In the end he became a victim of the very events he sought to reveal. In 1940 he and his family were trapped in the Netherlands when the Nazis invaded and he died in Auschwitz in 1944.

Salomon's photography refined that of the Edwardian snapper, building upon the public appetite for unposed naturalism. Within its first thirty years, photojournalism had established its métier. It offered a heady blend of the candid snap-shot, sometimes capturing moments of unfolding drama, with the negotiated photo opportunity and the stage-managed photograph, choreographed to give the illusion of spontaneity.

The photographer, at first consigned to the lower ranks of journalism, began to rise steadily within the newspaper hierarchy. Some of the best images, offered initially as transient message-carriers, began to linger in the memories of readers and to define the public's relationship with the previously remote world of the most famous and powerful.

King George VI and Queen Elizabeth at a mobile canteen, London, 1 October 1940

J.A. Hampton, Topical Press Agency

The otherwise shy and diffident 'Bertie' was suddenly thrust into the spotlight as George VI by the abdication of his brother Edward. The royal couple's understated resolve as the Second World War erupted all around them struck the right note with a population enduring the onslaught of the Blitz. Press photographs showing them chatting to staff at mobile canteens and visiting bomb-damaged homes in the East End and hospitals throughout London provided the ideal counterpoint to an image of the monarchy as remote and aloof.

Crowd reading notice of the execution of William Joyce (Lord Haw-Haw), Wandsworth Prison, London, 3 January 1946

J. Wilds, Keystone Press

Born in Brooklyn, New York, in 1906 to Anglo-Irish parents, William Joyce was a British passport-holder who supported Hitler. He first came to the public's attention as Director of Propaganda for Oswald Mosley's British Union of Fascists before re-emerging as the voice of wartime German radio propaganda. His broadcasts began with the words 'Germany calling, Germany calling', and were greeted in Britain with a mixture of ridicule and disgust. The name Lord Haw-Haw was coined by the radio critic of the *Daily Express*. Joyce was captured at the end of the war, tried for treason and hanged at Wandsworth Prison.

**Celebrating the Queen's return,
London, 1 May 1954** (OPPOSITE)

John Chillingworth, *Picture Post*

A young Prince Charles was featured on
the front page of the *Sunday Express*,
waving to his parents as they returned to
a wet and dour London spring. Royal tours of
the Commonwealth became media events,
photographed and filmed and offered to
the public back home as evidence of the
carefully managed withdrawal of Empire.

**Lady Diana Spencer and the press,
London, 13 May 1980**

Ian Tyas, Keystone Press

As a nineteen-year-old part-time assistant
at the Young England Kindergarten, Pimlico,
Diana Spencer was ill-prepared for the
media onslaught that greeted news of her
blossoming relationship with Prince Charles.
Followed every time she left her flat or got
in or out of her car, she was also persuaded
while at work to pose for the press, who
promptly lined her up against the morning
sun so it shone through her skirt and
silhouetted her legs. Shy Di, as she was
dubbed, soon cottoned on and in time
became an astute player of the media,
knowing just how and when to eclipse
her husband.

4 Breaking and making news

As the situation in Baghdad deteriorated into widespread looting and the pillaging of museums in 2003, US Secretary of Defense Donald Rumsfeld responded to questioning at a Pentagon press conference with the remark, 'Stuff happens.' Well, 'stuff' does indeed happen: big, banner-headline, unpredictable events that shatter our delusions of peace and set our nerves on edge, such as Chernobyl, the death of Diana, 9/11; events that have us switching on our televisions, swivelling from our workstations to our Internet browsers and, the next day, slowly trying to comprehend the enormity and finality of it all as we leaf through the special editions of the papers. But in truth big events happen fairly infrequently. They are by their very nature out of the ordinary. Daily newspapers are more concerned with items of transitory interest and ephemeral distractions.

Piers Morgan, former editor of the *Daily Mirror*, constantly confronted the detractors of modern tabloid journalism, who were forever evoking what he caricatured as the lost 'glory days of crusading, campaigning, investigative journalism'. Morgan took delight in marking the retirement of one of the *Mirror*'s seasoned journalists by digging out the edition that had been produced on the day, in 1961,

when the reporter joined the paper. Holding it aloft to what he described as a 'room packed with ex-*Mirror* hacks who spend all their time boozily bemoaning the fact it ain't what it used to be', he airily announced:

> Ladies and gentlemen, the first three pages were devoted to a house fire in which nobody died, but three stars of the Carry On movies were guests. Page five was an exclusive on Charlie Drake quitting showbiz because he's exhausted. Page nine was an interview with Zsa Zsa Gabor. There was a nice scantily clad woman on page eleven, a twelve and thirteen centre spread on the *Mirror*'s TV awards, three pages of sport and a back-page lead on Princess Margaret learning to swim.

(Piers Morgan, *The Insider: The Private Diaries of a Scandalous Decade*, Ebury Press, 2005)

Photography provided ideal illustrative fodder to pad out such mundane fare. Before and after the war, on an average day, photographers would be sent to cover an often unremitting diet of stake-outs, routine press calls and photo opportunities. Humphrey Spender, the documentary photographer for Mass Observation in the 1930s, worked briefly as the *Daily Mirror*'s 'Lensman' and recalled the jobs

the photographers hated most. On slow news days, when there were too few assignments to go round, they would be called in by the picture editor, one by one, from the back room where they waited, playing dominoes and drinking tea, and be given a job from the picture desk diary. The practice had developed, initially as a result of the growing number of specialist picture agencies, of keeping a diary in which annual events such as the January sales, maypole dancing, hop picking and bank holidays could be noted, as a reminder that there were always generic stories to be followed and filed on any day of the year. Newspapers and picture agencies unwittingly conspired to help construct a rigid, repetitive but potent image of regional and national identity from the necessity of keeping otherwise idle press photographers busy.

Sport could always be relied upon to provide not just a regular diary fixture but, with designated pages to fill, the increased probability of a picture sale. The increased readership of daily papers coincided with the rise, in the early twentieth century, of spectator sport as a mass leisure activity. The one seemed to feed the other. Towns and cities that had swollen as a result of industrial activity could all boast new sporting stadiums built either side of the First World War: athletics tracks, cycling velodromes, cricket grounds, greyhound stadiums, boxing halls and, above all, football grounds. The matches, races and games were reported in the press and readers came flooding in, attracted by the idea of being, if not at the event itself, at least close to the action.

Football, professionalized in 1885 and organized into leagues in 1888, grew rapidly in popularity. Dirt-banked slopes where spectators stood behind the goal were replaced with concrete terraces to accommodate demand. Liverpool's Kop, built in 1906, could hold 24,000; Aston Villa's Holte End, 30,000. Many of the fans were first-generation migrants to the cities and through football found a means to affirm their newly forged sense of com-munity. Pride in their team grew all the greater if success catapulted match coverage from the pages of the local papers to the nationals.

The sudden-death drama of the FA Cup attracted the biggest crowds. About 50,000 were expected for an FA Cup tie between Bolton and Stoke City in 1946, but 85,000 turned up. In the ensuing crush thirty-three fans were killed. With its capacity to generate conjecture and debate about events on and off the field, football seemed to hold the ingredients to fill more than just the back pages. The players themselves became stars, and if they were not instantly recognizable they were at least uncannily familiar.

In 1924 the spirit photographer Ada Emma Deane produced an image taken at the Cenotaph Armistice Day parade that purported to reveal the ghostly apparitions of dead soldiers. This was published as genuine in the *Daily Sketch* but abruptly pulled from distribution by a picture agency when it was noticed that many of the faces were those of journeymen footballers still playing in the league.

In reality, outside the enchanted circle of ghosts and fairies, there were few instances when the veracity of the press photograph was called into question. A news photograph was accepted for what it was. Few readers noticed the sometimes blatantly obvious puppeteer's strings in images that purported to tell the truth, but were in fact either works of fiction or at best recreations of events. One of the most telling examples, rich in the underlying complexities of the news agenda, is Fred Morley's image of a milkman picking his way though the devastation of a London street at the height of the Blitz in October 1940 (pages 80–81). The picture has been reproduced at regular intervals since the war, held up as an emblem of the country's defiance. At the time very few photographs depicting bomb

damage managed to get past the censors. Frustrated by the restrictions, Morley dressed his assistant as a milkman and had him walk though the ruined street. Block out the apparently chipper delivery-man and the surrounding scene provides one of the most graphic descriptions of wartime destruction. In order to tell a greater truth, the photographer simply created a more palatable fiction.

While pictures could be bent to the will of news-papers, it became obvious fairly early on that news could be shaped to meet the needs of photographers. In the first decades of the twentieth century, the women's suffrage movement was by any standards a major story. However, the increasingly audacious acts of public protest instigated by the Pankhursts' Women's Social and Political Union (WSPU) had potency only if they were reported in the press. The WSPU stressed to its supporters the value of publicity, encouraging them to 'conduct the biggest publicity campaign ever known. Make it more colourful and more commanding of attention than anything ever seen before' (Marian Ramelson, *The Petticoat Rebellion: A Century of Struggle for Women's Rights*, Lawrence and Wishart, 1967). No act of window smashing, rail chaining or palace storming would be attempted without first contacting the press, encouraging them to send along both their reporters and, more importantly, their photographers.

Coverage in the likes of the *Daily Mirror* and *Daily Express* ranged from the empathetic to the openly hostile, but publicity at any cost was seen as paramount. The lengths to which the suffragettes were prepared to go were underscored by Emily Davison when she died after throwing herself in front of the King's horse, Anmer, at the 1913 Derby. Emmeline Pankhurst described the act as being 'in full view of the King and Queen and a great multitude of their majesties' subjects', neglecting to mention the assembled ranks of press photographers, for whom the Derby was a key event in the sporting calendar (see page 59) and through whom an even greater and more significant multitude would bear witness to Davison's suicidal sacrifice. James Jarché recalled that as he and the other photographers trailed back to London: 'We saw a placard, "Suffragette killed at Epsom". We stopped to buy a paper to see what had happened. None of us had seen the incident. But when Pleat developed his plates he discovered that he had shot at the psychological moment, just before the horses trampled her' (James Jarché, *People I Have Shot*, Methuen & Co., 1934).

Being seen to act, oblivious of danger and before the lens of a camera, had obvious political potency. William Gladstone, who was prime minister four times, was one of the first to exploit the propaganda potential of photography, routinely outscoring the camera-shy Disraeli by posing for commercially available cabinet cards, sleeves rolled up, axe in hand, chopping logs on his Welsh estate. A generation on, Winston Churchill grasped the greater power of the popular press.

On 16 December 1910 the Metropolitan Police disturbed Russian and Latvian anarchists tunnelling into a Houndsditch jeweller's. The gang shot their way out, killing three policemen before escaping. Two weeks later they were eventually tracked down to Sidney Street in the East End. Police and press rushed to the scene. James Jarché was again an early arrival and found himself joined, shortly after, by Winston Churchill, who was then Home Secretary. Jarché recalled just how dangerous and unstable the situation was: 'I was standing in a gateway asking a police officer some questions, when suddenly blood spurted from the man's cheek. He had been hit by a bullet which had ricocheted off the wall.'

Held to have been reckless, Churchill was challenged by Arthur Balfour in the House of Commons

to explain how he came to be photographed there: 'I understand what the photographer was doing, but what was the Right Honourable gentleman doing?'

Of course, politicians never had things entirely their own way. Like any public figure, they emerged as blank canvases onto which wily photographers could project either a positive or a negative message. During his time on the staff of the *Daily Express* in the early 1960s, Harry Benson was assigned to cover the Tory Party conference at Brighton. During a break in the session he was taking tea in the hotel when he noticed Sir Hugh Fraser and his wife, Antonia, loitering in the foyer, where they were soon joined by Lord Jellicoe and Lord Hailsham.

Benson tailed them from the hotel to the beach. At a distance he photographed them in the awkward ritual of hopping on the pebbles while undressing beneath a beach towel. Fraser spotted him and came over to appeal to his better nature: 'I can't stop you showing pictures of us splashing about, but give me your word you won't publish pictures of us undressing.' Benson gave him his word, but when he returned to his hotel he found a stream of messages demanding that he call the office. He was put straight through to Lord Beaverbrook. Fraser, it seemed, had taken the view that he should 'get on to the Beaver and straighten things out'. Beaverbrook pronounced his verdict: 'You know Fraser didn't

Members of Broadstairs Council ready for gas drill, Kent, 29 November 1938

Reggie Speller, Fox Photos

The period between the Munich Agreement of September 1938 and Britain's declaration of war on Germany in September 1939 was one of increasing tension and preparation for what might lie ahead. With the horrors of the First World War still fresh in people's minds, it was feared that the Germans might drop poison gas by air. Some 38 million gas masks had been issued to civilians by 1940. Schools and local councils led the way in instructing people on their proper use and gas and air-raid drills became a part of daily routine.

have to get in touch with me. Your word was good enough. But now he has I'm inquisitive to see what you have. Send everything to London and we'll make that decision.' Benson complied. The next day pictures of the Tory leadership undressing on the beach were splashed across the front page of the *Daily Express*. When Fraser next spotted the photographer at the conference he headed straight over and said: 'Do you know what you are, Benson? You're a cad.' *

While those behind events might conspire to have them photographed and while photographers might chance upon photo-worthy events, just occasionally a photographer is the cause of an event. Kent Gavin, the one-time royal photographer of the *Daily Mirror*, was assigned to take pictures of Doris Day in her eighth-floor New York apartment. Thanks to Piers

Morgan's *The Insider*, what happened next has become one of the legends of Fleet Street. The story goes that while Doris Day answered a phone call the photographer was left alone with her pet dog. He started throwing a ball around for it to fetch. When he inadvertently threw the ball out of the window, to his horror the dog followed. Admitting to having witnessed a terrible accident, he then trailed the sobbing superstar down to the street, where she scooped up and cradled her deceased pet. 'I thought I may as well take a few pictures while I was there,' he confessed. Next day's *Daily Mirror* carried the world exclusive: 'Doris Day weeps for Dead Dog (pictures by Kent Gavin)'.

* This information is from interviews the author conducted with Harry Benson in New York in 2006.

Winston Churchill and Brendan Bracken surveying bomb damage, London, 11 May 1941

(PREVIOUS PAGE)

Keystone Press

A German air raid on 10 May 1941 started fires in the Houses of Parliament that destroyed the Commons Chamber and caused the ceiling in the Members' Lobby to collapse. Brendan Bracken was born in Ireland to a Catholic family with strong Republican ties, but he rose to power as a Conservative politician in the British government. He was a close friend and confidant of Winston Churchill. As Minister of Information between 1941 and 1945, he kept a watchful eye on Fleet Street, organizing teams of censors to study newspaper photographs and copy and weed out anything that might compromise security or erode morale.

Milkman delivering after German raid, London, 9 October 1940

Fred Morley, Fox Photos

From 7 September 1940 Germany began a bombing campaign over London that, in its first phase, continued for fifty-seven consecutive days. The Blitz frayed the nerves of everyone in the capital. How to report the all too evident carnage without undermining morale was a dilemma, particularly for photographers. Any image of death or large-scale destruction was suppressed by the censors. Fred Morley overcame the problem by persuading his assistant to dress as a milkman and chirpily pick his way through the rubble. The censors were satisfied and readers could see the true nature of the devastation by looking beyond the figure in the foreground.

Fleet Street reporters at Scotland Yard, London, 17 May 1947 (PREVIOUS PAGE)

Bert Hardy, *Picture Post*

Crime has always helped to sell popular newspapers. Thankfully, audacious bank robberies and gruesome murders are infrequent events, but when they do occur their discovery, investigation and the final prosecution provide reporters with plenty of material. The relationship between the press and the police has always been a tense, suspicious affair. On the one hand, publicity can generate vital information; on the other, the police are not keen on public scrutiny and are wary of revealing their cards too early in the investigative game. Bert Hardy's photograph for *Picture Post* shows two reporters camped out in Scotland Yard.

John Haigh arriving at Horsham Magistrates' Court, Sussex, 1 April 1949

Arthur Barrett, Press Association

Press pictures taken 'on the hoof', among groups of jostling photographers, are seldom perfect and are routinely cropped to include only the most essential details. The reduced pictures, when they appear on the page, have a hard-boiled quality that is further enhanced by pithy captions and attention-grabbing headlines. The young, handsome former cathedral choirboy John Haigh may have been everyone else's worst nightmare when the evidence of his six murders first emerged, but in the months between his arrest and his eventual execution he became the newspaper editors' dream. He claimed to have drunk the blood of his six victims before dissolving their bodies in sulphuric acid and was dubbed both 'the Vampire of London' and 'the Acid Bath Murderer'.

**John Christie arriving at
West London Magistrates' Court,
8 April 1953**

Keystone Press

In 1953 new tenants moved into 10 Rillington Place, the former home of John Christie. Attempting to trace the source of an unpleasant smell, they peeled back paper covering a hollow wall and discovered a woman's legs. Christie had been the chief prosecution witness against fellow Rillington Place tenant Timothy Evans, who was hanged in 1950 for the murder of his wife, Beryl, and their child. Christie, it later transpired, had murdered six women, including his own wife. The suspicion that he was also responsible for the Evanses' deaths encouraged public debate about the death penalty. Christie was hanged in July 1953. The death penalty was suspended in 1964 and Evans granted a posthumous pardon in 1966.

Lord Hailsham swimming at Brighton, 11 October 1957

Terry Fincher, Keystone Press

A shameless publicist, Lord Hailsham was happy to be photographed swimming in the sea during a break from the 1957 Conservative Party conference. He was leader of the House of Lords when Harold Macmillan announced his surprise retirement in 1963 and promptly renounced his peerage, hoping to become the next prime minister. He was re-elected to the House of Commons at a by-election as Quintin Hogg, but his attempt to become leader failed. Various antics, such as being photographed bottle-feeding his newborn baby and distributing 'Q' badges to conference delegates, alienated the party's grandees, leading them to prefer the more sober Alec Douglas-Home.

**John Profumo arriving at the
House of Commons, London,
26 October 1962**

Unknown photographer

As Secretary of State for War, John Profumo
was the key public figure to be sitting atten-
tively alongside the Prime Minister Harold
Macmillan as he read a statement on the
Cuban Missile Crisis. The stand-off between
Russia and the United States over the deploy-
ment of nuclear missiles in Soviet-friendly
Cuba precipitated one of the most chilling
moments of the Cold War when all out
nuclear war appeared as a distinct possibility.
It was in this climate that Profumo embarked
on a dangerous liaison that would be seen as
compromising British security.

Stephen Ward rushed to hospital, London, 31 July 1963

Aubrey Hart, *Daily Mirror*

Stephen Ward's dual career as a society fixer and an osteopath whose client list included Sir Winston Churchill and Elizabeth Taylor came crashing down in the wake of the Profumo scandal. Having arranged for call girls, including Christine Keeler and Mandy Rice-Davies, to party at Viscount Astor's Cliveden estate, Ward was charged with living off immoral earnings. On the last day of his trial, 31 July 1963, he took an overdose of sleeping pills. The press trailed him out of the ambulance and, while still in a coma, he was found guilty in his absence and died three days later.

Mandy Rice-Davies and Christine Keeler leaving the Old Bailey, London, 22 July 1963 (OVERLEAF)

Evening Standard

When news finally broke that Christine Keeler had had affairs with both John Profumo, the Conservative Secretary of State for War, and Yevgeny Ivanov, a naval attaché at the Soviet Embassy, the press went into overdrive. The scandal had the perfect ingredients for ever more salacious headlines as the tale of sex, politics and espionage at a famous country house unfolded. Mandy Rice-Davies provided the story's most memorable one-liner. Under cross-examination during the trial of Stephen Ward after it was put to her that Lord Astor denied having had an affair with her or even having met her, she quipped, 'Well, he would, wouldn't he?'.

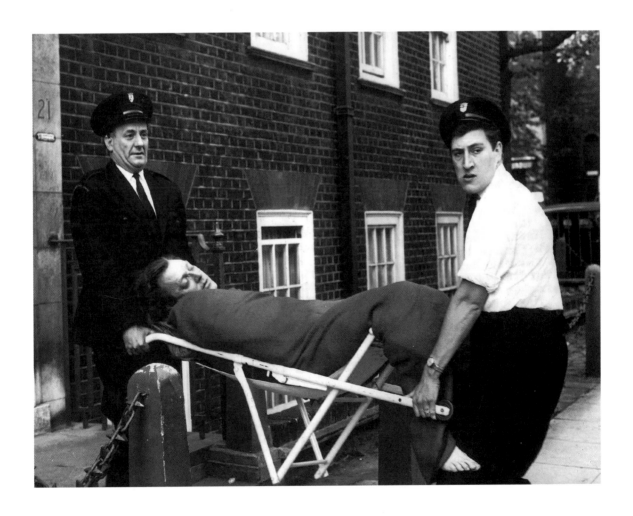

**Soccer air tragedy, Munich,
7 February 1959**

Daily Mirror

Tragedy was an entirely appropriate headline
for this edition of the *Daily Mirror*, reporting
the death of twenty-one of the forty-three
passengers on a flight chartered by the
Manchester United football team for their
return from a European Cup match in Belgrade.
Eight players and eight journalists died in the
accident, including the precociously talented
Duncan Edwards, who died fifteen days later,
and Frank Swift, the former England and
Manchester City goalkeeper who was working
for the *News of the World*.

**World Cup triumph,
Wembley, London, 30 July 1966**

Evening Standard

The image of captain Bobby Moore lifting
the trophy and hoisted onto his team mates
shoulders has become embedded in our
national consiousness as well as being cast
into bronze outside the ground of his former
club West Ham United. Once it was a freshly
minted image on a contact sheet offered,
in all probability, still wet, to an eager picture
editor to mark up and make a choice. The
nation's front pages are still awaiting a repeat
of this glorious success.

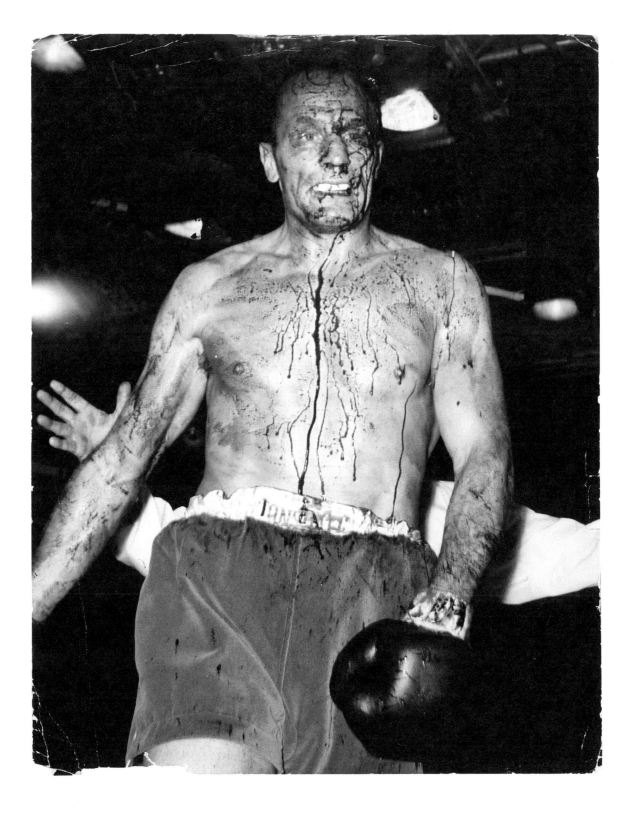

Henry Cooper, London, 21 May 1966

(OPPOSITE)

BIPPA Picture Agency

Henry Cooper was battered and bloodied when his rematch against Muhammad Ali, the world champion, at Arsenal's Highbury Stadium was stopped after six rounds. Ali's renouncement of what he derided as his slave name, Cassius Clay, and his refusal to fight in the Vietnam War forced him to contest all his 1966 fights outside the United States. Three years earlier, Cooper had floored Clay with his left hook at their first meeting at Wembley Stadium. Unfortunately for Cooper, the knockout came in the dying seconds of the fourth round and Clay was able to recover during the break, going on to win the fight.

Ronald Kray toasting Reggie Kray and Frances Shea at their wedding, London, 1 April 1965

Norman Potter, *Daily Express*

The Kray twins, whose property and nightclub empire had been built up through extortion, robbery and arson, were the most notorious London gangsters of the 1950s and 1960s. They flirted with publicity and enjoyed the company of celebrity friends. The press were invited to the wedding of Reggie Kray and Frances Shea, at which David Bailey acted as official photographer. The marriage lasted just eight weeks and Frances later committed suicide. The twins were eventually sentenced to life imprisonment at the Old Bailey in 1969.

John Lennon and Yoko Ono leaving court, London, 19 October 1968
Evening Standard

John Lennon first met Yoko Ono at her Exhibition #2 at the Indica Gallery, London. More used to rock stars having models and hairdressers as their lovers, the British press were at first bemused by the appearance of an older Japanese conceptual artist. Having left his wife, Cynthia, and their child at the family home in Weybridge, Surrey, John moved with Yoko into Ringo Starr's flat in Montagu Square, Marylebone. While there they were raided by the police and charged with possession of cannabis resin. A week after the court case Lennon divorced Cynthia.

Edward Heath, Jeremy Thorpe and Harold Wilson, Westminster Abbey, London, 27 July 1970

Fox Photos

From the mid-1960s to the mid-1970s these three men dominated British politics. The Liberal Party, under the leadership of Jeremy Thorpe, remained rooted in third place behind Labour and the Conservatives. Harold Wilson was Labour prime minister three times in this period and Edward Heath Conservative prime minister twice. The three leaders were portrayed by the press in very different ways. Wilson was the pipe-smoking, raincoat-wearing, working-class northerner made good; Heath the piano-playing, accident-prone bachelor yachtsman; and Thorpe the dandified enigma with a hint of darkness. The three had come together here for the unveiling ceremony of a memorial to Lloyd George.

Alfred Hitchcock with news of another necktie strangling, London, July 1971

Evening Standard

Feigning mock horror at the headline news of another necktie strangling eighteen years after John Christie's death, Alfred Hitchcock was in fact crafting Anthony Shaffer's script based on the 1950s murders into his penultimate film, *Frenzy* (1972). The plot hinged on the classic Hitchcock conceit of an innocent man framed by the true murderer and mirrored the case of Christie, whose story had been made into the 1971 film *10 Rillington Place*, starring Richard Attenborough. The press's theatrical billing of necktie stranglers and acid-bath murderers often embedded the stories in people's minds, ripening them for future film and television treatments.

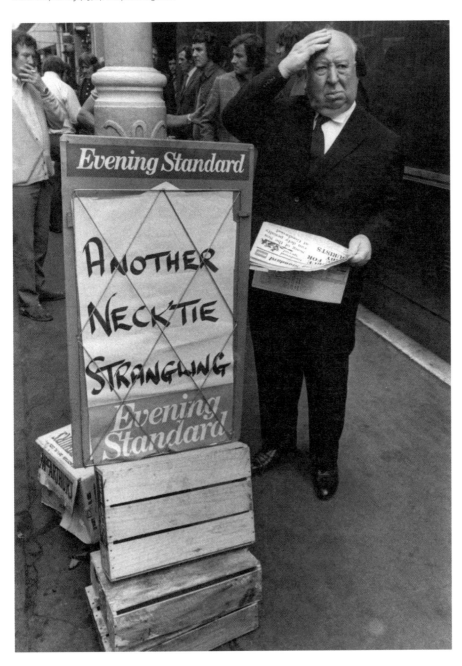

5 The end of Fleet Street

In 1960 *Life* magazine grandly proclaimed its prominence as a showcase for photojournalism by publishing a group shot of its thirty-nine staff photographers. The *Daily Express*'s Harold Keeble, realizing that he had as many photographers on call and not to be outdone, published a similar line-up in his own paper. Lord Beaverbrook was reported to have taken one look at the photograph and concluded it was graphic evidence, if any were needed, of chronic overstaffing.

Keeble was prominent among a number of newspaper art directors in the 1960s who took photography more seriously, investing in better picture placement and more considered selection. He encouraged younger photographers, mixing their work in a blend of hard-edged news photography and stylized fashion shots. In the early 1960s the broadsheet Sunday newspapers added colour supplements to their editions and opened the door to larger-budget assignments and photo shoots, inviting in photographers from America and creating opportunities for British photographers to establish international reputations. However, the interest in photography was neither entirely journalistic nor altruistic. In an early editorial meeting at the *Telegraph* magazine, which was originally published on a Friday, it was noted that advertisers who were commissioning expensive colour spreads were also demanding that the standard of the surrounding editorial photography be raised. At this point the production budget was increased and a novel style of news magazine created.

But for all the changes wrought on the surface of the papers, the underlying industry was mired in the grip of restrictive practices imposed by the powerful print unions. Disputes and wildcat strikes became common in the 1960s, escalating into the next decade (pages 101 and 102–3). In 1976 the *Nottingham Evening Post* attempted to introduce direct input by photojournalists and became embroiled in industrial action. In 1978 publication of *The Times* and the *Sunday Times* was suspended for eleven months, weakening the company and opening the way for its acquisition in 1981 by Rupert Murdoch's News International.

In 1982 Manchester businessman Eddy Shah, owner of a group of Warrington-based free newspapers, the Stockport Messenger Group, became the first media owner to test the Conservative government's recently implemented trade union reforms. Having sacked a handful of workers for joining the printers union, the National Graphical

Lord Goodman and Lord Thomson leaving No. 10 Downing Street, London, 12 June 1970

Michael Webb, Keystone Press

Lord Goodman (left) and Lord Thomson (right) are seen here leaving Downing Street after a meeting with the Prime Minister during the newspaper strike. Leading lawyer Lord Goodman held a number of chairmanships, including the Newspaper Proprietors'

Association. Lord Thomson owned *The Times* and the *Sunday Times*. In the 1950s and 1960s newspaper owners would do anything to avoid disrupting production. By 1970, as automation and computerized input became standard on provincial papers, the Fleet Street print unions dug in, resisting change and, in an effort to preserve jobs, insisting that their members should oversee the new technology. In effect this meant qualified operatives sitting alongside machines with nothing to do.

How the papers came back
Evening Standard
SO, IT'S GOOD
MORNING TODAY!
the papers came back

Association, Shah faced massed picketing and demonstrations outside his plant. His intransigent stand tested and weakened the hand of the union creating the opportune moment for Rupert Murdoch to take things further and force the unions to breaking point.

When Murdoch first gained his grip on Fleet Street with the acquisition of the *News of the World* in 1969, he declared, 'Anyone interested in journalism and mass newspapers realizes that Fleet Street is the heart of it all.'

In 1986, with his empire swollen to include the *Sun*, *The Times* and the *Sunday Times*, he didn't so much stab the industry in the heart as surgically remove its still-throbbing organ. The overnight decampment to new presses in Wapping, built in conditions of utmost secrecy, was a swift and sudden transplantation to a wholly new body. The plant, surrounded by high walls and razor wire and dubbed Fortress Wapping, was equipped with technology that was revolutionary within the British press but was, by the time of the move and by the standards adopted in other parts of the world, almost obsolete.

Pitched battles erupted along Wapping Wall between demonstrators and mounted police,

swollen on one side by the mobilized ranks of Militant and the Socialist Workers Party and on the other by the hired hands of News International. The unions fought a desperate rearguard action to resist change and maintain the upper hand of entrenched demarcation and long-established restrictive practices. It was always going to be a losing battle, with Murdoch enjoying the support of the Thatcher government, which was both ideologically opposed to the power of trade unions and a complicit benefactor of Murdoch's editorial support. Once the passion and the fury had evaporated, so too did the once familiar newspaper titles, which one after another began to rapidly desert Fleet Street. The *Sunday Express* printed the last newspaper to be produced from Fleet Street in 1989.

In 2005 the last major news organization left Fleet Street when Reuters vacated their iconic Sir Edwin Lutyens building for newly wired premises in Canary Wharf that were more suitable and readily adaptable to the electronically driven demands of modern news management. The occasion was marked, at Reuters behest, by a service at St Bride's, Fleet Street, the Christopher Wren-designed church which had been adopted as the spiritual home of the

**Enoch Powell electioneering,
Wolverhampton, 9 June 1970**

Leonard Burt, Central Press

Enoch Powell studied classics at Cambridge
under A.E. Housman, an education that
informed his notorious 1968 'Rivers of Blood'
speech on race relations – he said he foresaw,
in Virgil's words, 'the River Tiber foaming
with much blood'. The speech was made in
Birmingham three days before the Race
Relations Bill was to be debated in Parliament.
Edward Heath sacked him from his Shadow
Cabinet the next day. Powell stood for the
Conservatives for the last time in 1970. It is
believed the unexpected surge of support
in the West Midlands, surrounding Powell's
constituency, helped them to a surprise
general election victory.

newspaper industry and had emerged as the
favoured location for the memorial services of
recently deceased journalists. The congregation
gathered to hear the last rites for a departed
industry and the reading by Rupert Murdoch of
Hymn in Honour of Our Ancestors from Ecclesiasticus
44: 1–15.

Let us now sing the praises of famous men,
our ancestors in their generations.

Murdoch intoned in his familiar gruff Australian
burr to the attentive assembly of some 250 reporters,
columnists, photographers, editors and media
executives:

The Lord apportioned to them great glory,
his majesty from the beginning.
There were those who ruled in their kingdoms,
and made a name for themselves by their valour;
those who gave counsel because they were
intelligent;
those who spoke in prophetic oracles;
those who led the people by their counsels
and by their knowledge of the people's lore;

they were wise in their words of instruction;
those who composed musical tunes,
or put verses in writing.

He continued, concluding with the closing lines:

their offspring will continue forever,
and their glory will never be blotted out.
Their bodies are buried in peace,
but their name lives on generation after generation.
The assembly declares their wisdom,
and the congregation proclaims their praise.

The irony of the executioner-in-chief coming to
bury their bodies in peace was lost on no one, least
of all, one suspects, Murdoch himself.

Today all that remains of the last vestiges of
a print industry in Fleet Street is a handful of staff
in a small office owned by the Scottish publisher
D.C. Thomson. In a final twist to a tale of struggle
between owners and employees along the fault lines
of wealth and class, Thomson's staff quietly work
away on the production of the children's comic
the *Beano* and with it the weekly adventures of
Desperate Dan and Lord Snooty.

**Aftermath of IRA car bomb, Donegall
Street, Belfast, 20 March 1972**

Stanley Matchett, *Daily Mirror*

Nineteen-seventy-two was the most violent
year on record in the history of Northern
Ireland with 472 people killed in what has
become known as the 'Troubles'. On 30 January
British troops fired into a crowd of civil rights
marchers killing fourteen Catholic civilians.
'Bloody Sunday' served only to harden the
resolve of the breakaway Provisional Irish
Republican Army (IRA) who rejected the
peaceful tactics of the civil rights movement.
On Monday 20 March they placed a 46kg (100lb)
gelignite bomb in Donegall Street in central
Belfast. It exploded shortly before noon,
killing six and injuring 147 others.

Dirty protest: interior of prison cell at the Maze, Long Kesh, 31 January 1979

Central Press

From 1976 Republicans convicted of terrorist offences in Northern Ireland were housed in specially constructed H blocks at Maze prison. In protest at the British government's refusal to grant them political status, they refused to wear prison uniform. Prison officers then refused them access to toilets. So began a war of attrition between prisoners and the authorities that ended with excrement-smeared cell walls. In 1988 Margaret Thatcher's government banned the broadcast of the voices of Sinn Fein representatives in an effort to starve them of 'the oxygen of publicity'.

Page 3 model delivering colour TV to British troops, Belfast, 1974

(OVERLEAF)

Arthur Steel, *Sun*

Rupert Murdoch's acquisition of the *Sun* in 1969 from IPC Mirror Group added a daily paper to the Sunday *News of the World* he had bought a year earlier. He immediately made the paper into a tabloid, invested in advertising and introduced the Page 3 pin-up, which went topless on its first anniversary in 1970. The donation of colour TVs to British troops in Belfast was a typical publicity stunt of the period, mixing jingoism, patriotism, TV and glamour models. The troops, together with their regimental goat, welcomed both the gift and the visiting models.

The Sex Pistols, London, 2 December 1976 (PREVIOUS PAGE)

Peter Vernon, *Daily Mirror*

The front page of the *Daily Mirror* featured a photograph of the Sex Pistols: (clockwise from top left) Glen Matlock, Paul Cook, Johnny Rotten and Steve Jones. Shown in a shower of beer froth beside the headline 'The Filth and the Fury!' 'Who are these punks?' the paper asked. This followed the group's infamous appearance the evening before on Thames Television's *Today* show, hosted by Bill Grundy. Invited to say something outrageous, Steve Jones managed a string of expletives before the credits rolled. One irate viewer, it was reported, was so incensed that he put his foot through his television screen.

Jeremy Thorpe arriving at the Old Bailey, London, 18 June 1979

Aubrey Hart, *Evening Standard*

The death of a dog triggered one of the murkiest scandals in modern British politics. Jeremy Thorpe, former Liberal Party leader, was tried for conspiracy to murder male model Norman Scott. The case came to light when Andrew Newton was convicted of shooting Scott's dog, Rinka. Scott claimed he was the victim of a murder attempt after making frequent claims about his alleged homosexual affair with Thorpe. Thorpe and three co-defendants were acquitted when the testimony of former Liberal MP Peter Bessell was undermined by revelations that he had agreed to sell his story to the *Sunday Telegraph* for a fee that would rise with a successful prosecution.

**Rupert Murdoch relaunches
the *Sun* as a tabloid, London,
17 November 1969**

Press Association

Despite continuing disputes with the
printers, the *Sun* and the *News of the World*
proved highly profitable under Rupert
Murdoch's ownership, enabling him to
expand his business interests in the United
States and paving the way for the 1981
acquisition of *The Times* and the *Sunday
Times* from the Thomson family. The *Times*
titles had already been severely undermined
by a year-long dispute that ended in late 1979.
The introduction of new technology was
always high on Murdoch's agenda and his
overnight move to Wapping in 1986 triggered
a mass exodus of newspaper titles from
Fleet Street.

**Fleet Street at night, London,
14 February 1947** (OVERLEAF)

Harold Clements

After the newspapers moved to the Docklands
the area in and around Fleet Street assumed
a new nighttime calm. Before the mid 1980s,
just as the rest of London would be closing
down for the night, Fleet Street would be
coming alive to a riotous cacophony of blazing
light, thunderous noise and congested streets.
The notorious pubs and wine bars which
enjoyed such caustic sobriquets as the Stab
in the Back, the Printer's Devil and the Mucky
Duck were crowded out with journalists
fighting for last orders. There was a whiff of
printer's ink in the air and the pavements
shook to the roar of the presses. Every side
street would be blocked with delivery lorries
as they loaded up and nudged out to get a
head start in the race for the night trains.

Index

Figures in *italics* refer to illustrations.

(c) refers to caption text, when main and caption text appear on the same page.

Abdication, the (1936) 58, 61, *62*
Ali, Muhammad 95
Anschütz, Ottomar 54, 56
Answers to Correspondence 40–41
Associated Press 34
Astor, John 38
Astor, Waldorf, 2nd Viscount 89
aviators, early *39*, *42–3*

Bailey, David 34, 48, 95
Baldwin, Stanley 12, *14*, 62, *63*
Balfour, Arthur 76–7
Barrett, Arthur 84
Beano 106
Beaton, Cecil 16
Beaverbrook, Max Aitken, Lord 38, 42, *44*, 45, *45*, 77–8, 100
Benson, Harry 77–8
Berliner Illustrierte Zeitung 67
Bessell, Peter 114
BIPPA Picture Agency 95
Blau, Tom 38
Blériot, Louis *39*
BlowUp (film) 48
Bracken, Brendan *79*, 80
Brady, Reg *102–3*, 104(c)
Broadstairs Council members (in gas masks) *78*
Brougham, Eleanor *66*, 67(c)
Burt, Leonard 105

Camera Press 38
cameras 54, 56, 61
Camrose, William Berry, Viscount 15, 38
celebrities *31*, *32–3*, *37*, *64*, 72, 78, *96–7*, *112–13*, 114
Central Press 14, 59, 61(c), 105, 109
Chamberlain, Neville 9, *10*, 38
Chaplin, Charlie *64*
Charles, Prince of Wales *70*, 71
Chillingworth, John 71
Christie, John *85*, 99
Churchill, Sir Winston 12, *13*, 45, 76–7, *77*, *79*, 80, 89
circulation, newspaper 41, *46–7*, 48
Citizen Kane (film) 40, 52
Clements, Harold 36, 115
Cook, Paul *113*, 114
Cooper, Henry *94*, 95
Cowan, John 48
Cowley, John 38
Creasey, John 30
crime photography 56(c), *57*, 84, *84*, *85*, 95
Criminal Justice Act (1925) 56(c)
Crippen, Dr Hawley Harvey 56(c), *57*

Daily Chronicle 18
Daily Express 9, 18, 23, 25, 36, 38, *42–3*, 45, 52, 58, 68, 76, 95, 100
Daily Graphic 12, 61(c)

Daily Herald 18, 38
Daily Mail 12, 18, 19, 41, 48, 58, *62*
Daily Mirror 12, 16, 18, 38, 41, 48, 52(c), *53*, 56, 58, 72, 76, 78, 89, 92, *92*, 108, 114
Daily Sketch 9, *10*, 38, 75
Daily Star 52
Daily Telegraph 15, 38, 100
Davis, H.F. 23
Davison, Emily 76
Day, Doris 78
Dean, Bob *32–3*, 34
Deane, Ada Emma 75
Dellow, Alex 30
Delma, Paul 106
Derby, The (1913) 76
Desborough, Lady (Ethel Grenfell) *66*, 67(c)
Diana, Princess of Wales 15, *71*
Dillard, Harrison 'Bones' *26–7*
Donovan, Terence 34, *35*, 48

Edward VII 56
Edwards, Duncan 92
Edward VIII 15, *15*, 58, 61, *61*, *62*
Elizabeth, the Queen Mother 15, *68*
Epsom Derby (1920) *59*
Esten, Jack 31
Evans, Timothy 85
Evening News 16, 41
Evening Standard 30, 89, 92, 97, 99, *101–3*, 104(c), 114

fashion photography 34, *35*, 48, *49*
Fincher, Terry 87
Fleet Street 11, *17*, 18(c), 22, 104, 106, 115, *116–17*
football 22, *23*, 74–5, *92*, *93*
Forester, C. S. 30
Fox Photos 22, 24, 34, 36, 64, 76, 78, 80, 98
Fraser, Sir Hugh 77–8
Frayn, Michael: *Towards the End of the Morning* 30
French, John 34
Frenzy (film) 99
Fyfe, Hamilton 18

Garai, Bert 38
Gavin, Kent 78
General Photographic Agency 18(c)
George V 15, 56, *59*
George VI *60*, 61(c), *68*
Gladstone, William E. 76
Goodman, Lord *101*

Haigh, John *84*
Hailsham, Quintin Hogg, Lord 77, *86–7*
Hampton, J. A. 68
Hardy, Bert 9, 48, 84
Harmsworth, Alfred *see* Northcliffe, Lord
Harmsworth, Esmond *see* Rothermere, 2nd Viscount
Harmsworth, Harold *see*

Rothermere, 1st Viscount
Hart, Aubrey 89, 114
Hearst, William Randolph 40, 54
Heath, Edward 36, *98*, 105, 106(c), *107*
Hill, Benny 30
Hitchcock, Alfred *99*
Hobsbawm, Eric 22
Hopkinson, Tom 56, 58
Howe, Anne 36
Hudson, Frank *32–3*, 34
Huxley, Elspeth 30

Ipswich Town football players *22*
IRA bombing (1972) *108*

Jameson, Derek 52(c)
Jarché, James 18, 76
Jenkins, Simon: *The Market for Glory* 104(c)
Jewish refugees *24*
Johnson, Amy *42–3*
Jones, Steve *112–13*, 114
Joy, Ken *9*
Joyce, William ('Lord Haw-Haw') 68

Karsh, Yousuf 12
Keeble, Harold 100
Keeler, Christine 89, *90–91*
Kemsley, Lord 38
Keystone Press Agency 15(c), 38, 68, 71, 80, 85, 87, 101, 106(c)
King, Peter 36
Kray, Reggie and Ronald *95*

Layton, Sir Walter 38
Lennon, John *96–7*
Life magazine 100
Lloyd George, David 12, *13*, 44, *55*, 56(c), 98
Lorant, Stefan 38, 61
LSD experiments *25*
Le Neve, Ethel *57*

MacDonald, Ramsay 62, *63*
Macmillan, Harold 87, 88

Martin, Paul 54
Matchett, Stanley 108
Matlock, Glen *112–13*, 114
Maxwell, Robert 44, 52, *53*
Maze prison, Long Kesh *109*
Mills, Ernest 56(c)
Mirror see Daily Mirror
Moore, Bobby 92, *93*
Morgan, Piers 72, 78
Morley, Fred 75, 80
Munich air crash (1959) *92*
Murdoch, Rupert 104, 106, 109, *115*

National Graphical Association 100, 104
New York Daily Graphic 16
New York Journal 40
New York Press 40
New York World 40, 41
News Chronicle and Star 38
News International 100, 104
News of the World 104, 109, 115
Nicholson, Keith and Viv *48*
Northcliffe, Alfred Harmsworth, Lord 12, 18, *39*, 40–41, 44, 45
Northern Ireland *108*, *109*, *110–11*
Nottingham Evening Post 100

Oberon, Merle *31*
Odhams publishing group 40
Olympic Games (London, 1948) *26–7*
Ono, Yoko *96–7*

Pankhurst, Emmeline *73*, 74(c), 75, 76
photo finishes *26–7*
Picture Post 9, 30, 38, 48, 56, 71, 84
politicians and political events 9, *10*, *13*, *36*, *55*, 56(c), 62, *63*, 76–8, *86–7*, *88*, 89, *98*, *101*, *105*, *106*, *114*
Popper, Paul 38
Potter, Norman 95
Powell, Enoch *105*
press agencies 22

Press Association 56(c), 74, 84, 115
press coach, Monte Carlo Rally *30*
press conferences *31*
Profumo, John *88*, 89
proprietors, newspaper 38, 40, 44, *45*, *46*, 52, *53*, 100, 104, 106, *115*
Pulitzer, Joseph 40, 41, 54

Reuters 104
Rice-Davies, Mandy 89, *90–91*
Rothermere, Esmond Harmsworth, 2nd Viscount 38, 40
Rothermere, Harold Harmsworth, 1st Viscount 40, 41, 45
Rotten, Johnny *112–13*, 114
Royal Family, the 15, *15*, 56, 58, *59*, 60, 61, *61*, 62, *68*, *71*
Rubinger, David 52(c)
Rumsfeld, Donald 72

Salomon, Erich 62, 67, 67(c)
Sapt, Arkas 41
Saroyan, William 30
Scherman, David E. 45
Sellers, Peter 36, *37*
Sex Pistols *112–13*, 114
Shaffer, Anthony 99
Shah, Eddy 100, 104
Shea, Frances *95*
Sickert, Walter 7
Sidney Street Siege (1911) 76, *77*
Simpson, Wallis 15, *15*, 58
Southwood, Lord 38, 40
Speller, Reggie 78(c)
Spender, Humphrey 72
sports events 9, *26–7*, *59*, 74, 76, *94*; *see also* football
Starr, Ringo 34
Steel, Arthur 109
Stevens, Jocelyn *102–3*, 104(c)
Stevenson, Frances 56(c)
suffragettes 19, *73*, 74(c), 75–6
Sun 18, 52, 104, 109, 115
Sunday Express *70*, 71, 104

Sunday Telegraph 114
Sunday Times 100, 101, 104, 115
Swaffer, Hannen 18
Swift, Frank 92

Taylor, Elizabeth 89
technical advances 16, 41, 54, 56
telephones, use of 23
Thatcher, Margaret 104, 106(c), *107*, 109
Thomson, D. C. 106
Thomson, Ken, Lord *101*
Thorpe, Jeremy *98*, *114*
Time & Life Pictures 45, 52(c)
Times, The 38, 100, 101, 104, 115
Titanic, sinking of the 19, *20–21*
Tocqueville, Alexis de: *Democracy in America* 15
Topical Press Agency 19, 22, 23, 39, 68
trade unions 1001, 104
Tyas, Ian 71

United States of America 40, 54

Vanderson, William 24
Vernon, Peter 114

Ward, Stephen *89*
Webb, Michael 101
Weekly Illustrated 61
Welles, Orson: *Citizen Kane* 40, 52
Wilds, J. 68
Wilson, Harold *36*, *98*
Women's Social and Political Union (WSPU) 74(c), 75–6
World War, Second 12, 16, 25, 67, 68, 75, 78(c), *79*, 80, *80–81*
World Wide 22

'Yellow Journalism' 40, 54

Zimmermann, Edward 76(c)

Director's acknowledgement

I would like to acknowledge all those who have also worked hard in the making of this project, most particularly Sophie Clark and Rosie Wilson, exhibitions managers, and this book's editor Caroline Brooke Johnson and designer Philip Lewis. I should also like to thank the proofreader Alison Effeny and indexer Vicki Robinson as well as colleagues at the National Portrait Gallery, especially Joanna Banham, Pim Baxter, Rob Carr-Archer, Naomi Conway, Andrea Easey, Shirley Ellis, Denise Ellitson, Neil Evans, Ian Gardner, Celia Joicey, Ruth Müller-Wirth, Terence Pepper, Jonathan Rowbotham, Jude Simmons, Jacob Simon, Sarah Tinsley, Pallavi Vadhia and Alexandra Willett and acknowledge the many others in the Communications and Development, Learning and Access and Exhibitions departments who have made the exhibition and publication possible.

SANDY NAIRNE

Curator's acknowledgement

I owe a particular debt of thanks for their patience and encouragement to the book's editor Caroline Brooke Johnson and the exhibition's managers Sophie Clark and Rosie Wilson. Any exhibition and book project involves a journey and might sometimes involve false starts and missed turnings and it's always useful to stop along the way and ask directions. At an early stage Philippe Garner and Michael Rand helped point the way forward. Jane Moore and Anne Braybon, two wonderfully talented picture editors, also provided essential advice. Not long before he died Humphrey Spender sketched out for me an evocative picture of Fleet Street in the 1930s while Harry Benson filled out the canvas for the 1950s and '60s with colour and verve.

Certain pictures and certain archives were suggested by Richard West of *Source* magazine and by Will Carlton whose Photo Archive News is emerging as a champion of the history of Fleet Street photojournalism. Sarah McDonald, gatekeeper of Getty Images' historic archives, has been mentioned elsewhere but should be mentioned again for her professionalism and knowledge. Fergus McKenna of Mirropix opened the way to pick through the collections of the *Daily Mirror*. I'd especially like to thank the team at the Press Association and EMPICS who were not only helpful but enthusiastic. Ian Blackwell of Popperfoto and the staff of the Berlinische Galerie, Berlin were also very helpful. Finally I'd like to thank the generations of press photographers, some of whose names have become detached from their pictures, who have provided both daily interest and a lifelong legacy that is only now coming to be appreciated.

ROGER HARGREAVES

Picture credits